LUST &
WONDER

Also by
Augusten Burroughs

LUST & WONDER

AUGUSTEN BURROUGHS

ST. MARTIN'S PRESS ⚏ NEW YORK

The names and identifying characteristics of some people have been changed.

www.stmartins.com

A portion of Part III first appeared in the "Modern Love" column of *The New York Times* on May 23, 2013.

Designed by Steven Seighman

The Library of Congress Cataloging-in-Publication Data is available upon request.

ISBN 978-0-312-34203-6 (hardcover)
ISBN 978-1-250-10103-7 (international, sold outside the U.S., subject to
    rights availability)
ISBN 978-1-250-09168-0 (limited edition)
ISBN 978-1-250-08236-7 (e-book)

Our books may be purchased in bulk for promotional, educational, or business use. Please contact your local bookseller or the Macmillan Corporate and Premium Sales Department at 1-800-221-7945, extension 5442, or by e-mail at MacmillanSpecialMarkets@macmillan.com.

First U.S. Edition: March 2016

First International Edition: March 2016

10 9 8 7 6 5 4 3 2 1

For Crsripley

I

Just when I broke my sobriety and started drinking again in moderate and controlled measure exactly like a normal person, I met this guy who wasn't just a guy but a writer, and not just a writer but the author of one of my favorite books.

In AA, you are brainwashed into believing that all the good stuff happens only after you stop drinking. Clearly they are lying; my life improved significantly as soon as I ordered a cocktail.

Our meeting was very romantic, at least by the gay standards of the mid-1990s. Which is to say not at a gym or in the midst of a spiraling blackout but through fan mail. I sent him a note:

> *Dear Mitch,*
> *Let me just say right off that I am not Kathy Bates in* Misery. *I do not have a double-headed axe or a criminal*

record. In fact, I was at my friend's apartment and saw a copy of your most recent book on his shelf. I pointed to it and said, "Isn't that the sickest, most wonderful novel, ever?" He explained that he hadn't actually read it but that you and he had gone out on a date six months ago and, for whatever reason, it just didn't work out. Which is how I got your e-mail address. I probably sound crazy, like a stalker. Like a "fan." But I'm really very normal, stable, healthy, and maybe even a little bit boring. If you're interested, write me back. I'm attaching a photo I took of myself just five minutes ago. And yeah, I do own shirts.

He replied almost instantly, like he'd been expecting to hear from me. "I'd love to meet you," he wrote. "You look great!"

The swiftness and brevity of his reply caused me to instantly resent him. I felt deprived of suspense and the luxurious anxiety of wondering if I'd made a fool of myself by attaching a shirtless photo with my stalker note.

Now he was the dish of wrapped peppermints next to the cash register that I didn't want because they were free.

Because his reply to my note expressed only his desire to meet me along with a compliment, I almost felt like I could have achieved the same result by sending no words at all; just the shirtless photo of me standing on my shabby terrace. It was even possible he had looked at my picture and then merely skimmed my carefully crafted e-mail.

And while it was true that I was working out for two hours every day so that I could have the kind of body that inspires in others a sickening feeling of jealousy and inferiority, it was also true that I, myself, looked down on people with such bodies and felt myself vastly superior to them. I would simply never date somebody with a body like mine; they would be too vapid.

I made-believe I didn't feel this way by once again studying the author photo on the back cover of his book. *But he's so handsome. And he's published!* These two qualities, when combined, seemed to detonate any developing sense of doubt.

Besides, just the fact that he *had* an author photo was enough.

I understood that I was clearly insane. But he apparently hadn't picked up on how many times in one short letter I asserted that I was *not*. This acceptance of my questionable mental health made me feel confident that we would be compatible, possibly for life.

I wrote him back right away and suggested we meet that very evening.

The restaurant where we met was located between our two apartments in the East Village and featured a great deal of pale-blue neon in the window, which stained us as we sat in our booth.

We each ordered a vodka martini, and he automatically offered me his olive, which I read as a very good sign. Olives are the wishbones of the cocktail world; rarely are they freely passed along to somebody else.

He blushed and averted his eyes when I praised his novel, seeming genuinely uncomfortable. This caused me to fawn even more, which in turn made him down the rest of his martini and signal the waiter for another.

It was a strangely powerful feeling to watch my words of praise disassemble his composure like that. Which is probably why I continued and elaborated in multiple directions by saying, "I love that you have a cleft chin," and "I think you look even better in person than in your author photo."

He asked about me, and I gave him a slightly sanitized version. "Well, I've been an advertising copywriter since I was nineteen. I'm freelance now, which is better because it's forced me to care less, and for some reason, this has improved the quality of my work."

I left out the fact that I'd been shoved into rehab a year and a half before because I was such a disaster, always missing meetings or showing up to them drunk, which was even worse.

When Mitch asked me about my family, I took a sip from my drink and said, "I've never been very close to them."

I had long ago learned not to unload all of my sordid past on somebody during the first date. I had done this very thing in the past, and it hadn't worked out well. When people find out your mother was mentally ill, your father was a chronic alcoholic, and you spent most of your childhood being raised by your parents' eccentric and possibly insane psychiatrist in his run-down mental hospital of a house, they tend to back away. In order to make them lean in and want more, I had to polish certain elements from my life, while omitting others entirely.

"My mother was a poet," I told him, leaving out the fact that she was a poet on antipsychotic medications and had been hospitalized throughout my childhood.

Mitch didn't press me for additional details about my

family. The only thing he wanted to know was, "How did you get into advertising at nineteen?"

I told him, "I was living in San Francisco," as though that would explain everything. Which, actually, it did.

Just before turning eighteen, I moved to Boston with the money I'd saved from being a Ground Round waiter, enrolling in a computer programming trade school called Control Data Institute. Just before I graduated nine months later, I saw the most hideous, downscale daytime TV commercial for my own school. It made me realize that I was most certainly not at MIT.

I was so mortified.

I thought, *Somebody thought of that. It came into their head, and they said, "Yeah."*

I realized I could think of a better ad than that one without even trying. Then to prove it to myself, I sat down with the only magazine in the apartment—a copy of *Fortune* that belonged to my roommate—and going page by page, I rewrote every ad in it.

The only paper I had to type on was the blank side of my programming flowchart paper from school, so I used that. As a result, my first "portfolio" was pink.

Then, because I didn't know (or care) any better, I started to call advertising agencies in Boston, asking if I could come in and show them my ads.

Every ad agency I contacted agreed to meet with me. That blew me away.

But the result was the same each time: humiliation. One

creative director sneered, "Um, ads have visuals? Not just words. Your spelling is just horrendous. And why do you have commas all over the place?"

It didn't help that my portfolio case was a paper bag. I was broke.

I was also totally over computer programming school. I cheated my way through the rest of it—not because it was difficult but because I needed to spend my coding time writing pretend ads for my ever-expanding portfolio.

Because now that I had decided on advertising, I was determined.

Each day, I would walk the four miles from where I was staying into Boston's business district. I didn't care about my feet. I didn't need a drink of water; the sweat would eventually evaporate, and I would eat something when I got home.

All that mattered was advertising. I had to get in.

Advertising came naturally to me. I could write fifty ads for the same can of tuna. What I didn't know was if even one of those ads was any good.

I was starting to worry the answer might be no. I'd arranged interviews with a dozen agencies, which I now knew were called "shops," and I couldn't shake the feeling that to most people, I was kind of an eccentric joke. Definitely not a copywriter.

The problem was, there were only a couple of agencies I'd failed to meet with. I was running out of options.

Then a creative director at one of these last-on-the-list ad agencies told me this: "Half of the words in this portfolio are incorrectly spelled. You overuse commas. These ads themselves look terrible, like each one has been touched by dozens of dirty hands. And there are about thirty ads too many here. It's good that you have range, but you can still demonstrate that with twelve to fifteen ads, total. And here's my last comment, and it's the big one."

I had long, curly hair and wore sunglasses twenty-four hours a day. I had a hoop earring like a pirate. I wore extremely baggy, deconstructed clothing at a time when the rest of the world was into zippers and Spandex. And I had now met with practically every agency in Boston and even a bunch of the stores, looking for something in-house.

This guy had been my last chance.

And here he was, just layering on "no" in a hundred different ways. I wanted to evaporate, not just leave his office. I didn't want any more of his words on me.

He leaned forward and looked at me with a strange intensity. It made me stop fidgeting, and it made me keep looking at him. But most of all, that gaze of his made me listen.

He said, "I understand that you may have limited finances, but let me tell you something. If you are going to walk into my office with a paper bag filled with ads—not even an inexpensive black portfolio case like you could pick up in Harvard Square for twelve bucks but a plain old brown paper bag—if you have the nerve to do that? Then the ads inside that paper bag had just better be the best ads I have ever seen in my life."

Well, he was right.

There was nothing I could say to him, because he was just right.

It didn't matter that I could never afford to spend twelve dollars on something that was not then digested. He was right. I was wrong.

But he continued, "And that is exactly the situation here. This is the best portfolio I have ever seen from a junior writer. And if one person tells you otherwise, that person is lying, because you have an obvious and enormous talent. You will get your job in advertising, but it won't be in Boston. This town is too conservative. You belong where they are doing the best work in the country—you belong in San Francisco."

With those words, that man changed my life. Because I didn't need to have enormous talent. Just enough to get me a job in advertising. The man had not given me hope; he had given me a surplus of it.

As it happened, a fellow graduate of the Control Data Institute was heading west. And when you are traveling from Boston to San Francisco by car, it's kind of great when your friend happens to be a car guy.

We did not pass one other Mercury Merkur XR4Ti the entire way. It was bulbous, nearly oblong, white, and fast with a spoiler in back that was more like a wing. It resembled no car ever seen on an American highway. In about four years, all new cars would feature these smooth, egg-inspired curves, but in 1985, it was as if we were driving across America in something from the distant future.

When we pulled into a gas station in Omaha, Nebraska, or Kalispell, Montana, every last person would stare.

From out of this curious, even worrisome pod of a car would step one normal guy and me: nineteen, usually barefoot, dressed like a half girl, wearing sunglasses, and out of my mind with excitement about my future.

I would look at the gawking farmers, dungaree-wearing good old boys, sandpapery ranch workers, and engine-stained mechanics, and I would smile at them and think to myself, *I could sell you panty hose.*

I loved the way that car punched you in the kidneys every time the turbo kicked in.

After all the detours, pit stops, and side trips, it would be a few weeks before we arrived in San Francisco. If my friend hadn't been so generous with his credit card, I would have been forced to walk most of that way.

But we did make it to San Francisco. And even when I am eighty-three years old and strapped to my foam mattress in the basement of a nursing home, I will never forget the surprise of San Francisco—the lusty, big-breasted, glittering, and thigh-slapping shock of it. I knew only one thing about San Francisco: it was where the gays lived.

Now I knew why.

If you are a kid who came from a garbage dump of a life and your feet have inch-thick calluses because even shoes feel oppressive and your hair is as long as you can grow it because it is fucking yours and you wear sunglasses all the time so that nobody can see your eyes and be able to tell that, despite all appearances to the contrary, you were carved from a solid block of goodness and kindness and grace but are now so ruined and so young that there is not one logical reason for anybody to believe you will ever be anything—somehow, you just know. You know. If you are this person, I happen to know from personal experience that San Francisco will not merely welcome you. San Francisco will give you the longest, hottest bath you have ever had. It will drape a fresh, white cotton shirt over your shoulders, and even though this shirt will be three sizes too big, it will fit you better than any shirt ever has or ever will. And once you are sitting in an overstuffed armchair that has been warmed for you by a cat, San Francisco will muss your hair. You will have some milk and one of those thick brownies with a shiny top that shatters when you bite it. And then, as you walk down the long hallway toward your bedroom, San Francisco's fishnet stocking–clad leg will suddenly rise up and block your way. San Francisco will smile and say, "Hon? Either brush those teeth or donate them to the pointy end of my boot." And you will brush your teeth and never have another cavity. Until you're forty. Then San Francisco will tuck you into bed like you are a baby, and this will not embarrass you at all. And even though you're nineteen, San Francisco will leave the light on; you won't even have to ask. And when you wake up, San Francisco will be the first thing you see when you open your eyes. And it will say to you, "You know it. And I know it. Get out there and make them see it."

The very first advertising agency to meet with me hired me. The creative director was unlike any I had ever seen back in Boston. This one dressed even more outrageously than I did, had way longer hair, and much, much longer nails, which were bright red.

I was in awe of her.

She loved advertising as much as I did, but she knew so much more. I was like her disciple, not her employee. I would sit in her office in the morning while she ate the top off her muffin, passing me the base.

"Never use the word *delicious*, because it doesn't mean anything anymore," she told me.

I did a lot of work at that agency, and some of it finally got attention from New York. Headhunters started to call and ask if I would be interested in flying out to meet with a few agencies.

I'd always wanted to live in Manhattan, but not as a poor, starving artist. Coming from San Francisco with some work under my belt, I'd be able to earn a respectable income. I loved San Francisco, but I knew I belonged in New York.

My first job was at a legendary agency named Ogilvy & Mather. But it was a real culture shock after the boutique-sized San Francisco agency. There was a lot of politics and backstabbing, not to mention a massive antique pub bar in the cafeteria.

Another difference was that people changed jobs with a lot more frequency in New York. That's how you got a raise. So after a couple of years, I hopped over to another agency and then another and then several more. My portfolio improved over the years, but I never had that sense of family I'd experienced in San Francisco. I never had another genius boss like Lynda.

I was very good at advertising, but being good at something wasn't necessarily a good reason to continue doing it. I no longer loved it; I didn't even like it. It was just the same day, over and over with different clients, different products. It wasn't fun anymore.

But I couldn't do anything else, and that was the problem.

At least I could do it freelance. If you loathe your job, the situation is improved if you can do it in your underwear. Drunk.

Several months after our first date, I was madly (mostly) in love with Mitch; it was just every single cliché and Whitney Houston song strung together into one endless, intolerable group hug.

Our relationship had reached the *key* stage.

Mitch was the one who brought it up, which was unexpected and refreshing, like walking into the kitchen after preparing a hurricane of a meal for a dozen people and finding it utterly, miraculously spotless.

We were standing and facing each other.

"Do you think it's too soon to exchange keys?" he asked. He had his hands in his pockets, and he rolled forward a little off his heels. This had the pleasing effect of making him seem magnetically attracted to me.

I hadn't even thought about exchanging keys, but when I did, I realized there was no such thing as "too soon." That was exactly the right moment to do it, and he was exactly the right guy to bring it up, gallantly sparing me.

"Not at all," I said.

He smiled and pulled one of his hands out of his pockets. He said, "Good, because . . ." and handed me a freshly minted brass key.

Mitch watched as I removed my own key ring and unsuccessfully tried to pry my thumbnail into the groove to open up enough space, so I handed it over to him. "Can you do this?"

"Oh yeah," he said, "I'm good at that." And he was. Because in like three seconds, it was done.

I reached for my wallet and found the spare key to my own apartment that I kept in a slot with my driver's license. I handed it over. "Maybe you can put this one on your own key ring while you're at it."

He was still smiling, but his smile grew even warmer, the dimples creasing both cheeks. "I love that you already have a spare with you. Like you were ready."

"Oh, I was ready," I told him. "I've been ready since I was nine."

It actually turned out to be a weirdly romantic little moment even though it only involved a base metal.

The great thing about exchanging keys is that it's just one or maybe two floors below the romance level of rings, and if things don't work out—or worse, go horribly wrong—you don't even have to ask for them back. All you need is a twenty-four-hour locksmith, and New York City probably has more locksmiths than rats.

I had stopped living according to the Gregorian calendar. Time passed in the form of dates with Mitch. Something happened not "last week" but rather "four dates ago," and, typically, everything that happened between us happened after several martinis.

Mitch was deeply odd, and this appealed to me enormously. The fact that he was my favorite author seasoned everything about him with a kind of positive-spin saffron. My initial infatuation, though, was burnished away by almost constant contact, and I began to notice small details. For example, I saw that he had fine lines around his eyes, which I hadn't seen before. I realized that until we traded keys and started sleeping over at each other's places, I'd only seen him at night in dim, flattering restaurant lighting.

The sun was not his friend.

The first morning we woke up together and I looked at his face, the phrase *ravaged by time* came to my mind. Of course, he rolled over and smiled and said, "I love this. I love waking up next to you."

I managed to smile back at him and say, "Oh, I know. Me too," but what I was really thinking was, *Now I need to go to a darkroom supply store and buy blackout shades for my apartment.*

Another thing I noticed once we started hanging out in the sunlight with hangovers instead of at midnight with cocktails was the patchy nature of his body hair. Most of his chest was covered with short, black hair except for areas where it appeared simply to have been worn away by some kind of unexplained friction. It was the same on his arms and legs. Although I hated myself for it, I thought it anyway: he looked used up already. Mentally, I demoted him to Secondhand Mitch, a spontaneous nickname that stuck the instant it entered my small, mean brain.

I probably could have overlooked every one of these things if only he hadn't insisted upon speaking. But all he could talk about was what a failure he was. Mitch was a bemoaner.

To me, it was a staggering accomplishment that he'd published two books. Mitch saw this as evidence of failure, because he'd written several others and none of them had found publishers. This became the only thing he talked about after the brief ceremony of exchanging keys. Dinner suddenly meant cocktails, pub burgers, and a tiresome diatribe against the publishing industry and the futility of his existence as a failed and talentless writer.

"I should just kill myself," he groaned. "I don't even deserve to be alive and eat burgers."

My feeling was, *But you do deserve to pay for them, that's for damn sure.* So when the check arrived, I stopped automatically reaching for my wallet.

It was actually quite stunning. The keys themselves had seemingly unlocked his negative, depressive nature and released it into the wild. I now suspected the wrinkles around his eyes were the result not of sunlight but rather scowling in misery for extended periods.

"I'll never have another book published again," he complained as he chewed fries. "I am *such* a loser. God, I hate my life."

I tried to be encouraging. "You're not a loser. It'll happen again, you'll see. And your last book was amazing. Don't forget, that's how we met."

But my efforts only made him feel worse.

"Oh my God, now I have to deal with your pity on top of everything else? You should get another boyfriend, somebody who's not defective like me."

"But I'm defective, too," I told him, reaching across the table for his greasy fingers. "I'm even more defective than you are, I promise."

Mitch's best friend was also a writer, but quite a famous one. They'd met in college, moved to the city together, and had lived practically next door to each other ever since.

He was a disarmingly sweet guy, exceedingly charismatic and funny. All of which was surprising given his reputation as a notorious egomaniac and douche-bag, known more for snorting coke off toilet lids than gentlemanly charm. I liked him a lot. He was good-looking. I might even describe him as *powerfully* good-looking. In fact, that's exactly how I would describe him.

He was also an excellent cook, which I discovered when Mitch and I went to his place for Thanksgiving and he prepared the turkey himself. That doesn't sound like much in itself, but the first time in your life you have Thanksgiving turkey that isn't dry, you just don't expect it to have come from the oven of an internationally bestselling novelist and fixture of Manhattan nightlife. I would have expected such a fine turkey from, say, Barbara Kingsolver. But not from this guy. So it was sort of a wow moment. Also, he looked dapper in a white chef's apron.

There were lots of people there, including several celebrities, but I found myself most engaged by Famous Author Friend and could only look away from him with effort.

He held court majestically at his concrete-topped dining table, telling witty and unflattering stories about his celebrity acquaintances while Mitch just kind of melted back into his chair, shrinking and glowering and not saying much of anything except to occasionally interject himself into the conversation in order to argue a small and irrelevant fine point.

"And then she grabbed her Tony off the shelf and used the base to hammer the hook into the wall!"

"It wasn't a Tony," Mitch mumbled petulantly as he stared at the serving plate of buttered peas in the center of the table. "It was a Daytime Emmy."

Famous Author Friend glanced over at him like, *Dude, really?*

The cleft in Mitch's chin that I'd previously admired and considered one of his best features suddenly became an asshole on his face.

After we left, anxious Mitch seemed genuinely relieved, exhaling in the elevator, as though we'd escaped just barely in time, right before the electric chair was dragged out from the coat closet.

I, on the other hand, felt like we'd left the party too soon. I thought we should have stayed, perhaps even long after everyone else had left. I could have cleaned up.

On the walk to the inevitable bar, Mitch admitted that he'd had trouble in the past introducing boyfriends to Famous Author Friend, because they always ended up wanting to date *him* instead of Mitch. Apparently, Mitch lost two or three boyfriends in precisely this fashion.

I could immediately see what the problem was, of course: in addition to avoiding daylight, Mitch should never be seen in the same room at the same time with his friend. When you could compare them side by side like that, Famous

Author Friend did come across as infinitely more exciting, appealing, and desirable. Much like thinking your own engagement ring is lovely until you see Elizabeth Taylor's.

While I could no longer tell myself that I was drinking moderately like a normal person, my drinking didn't seem to be a problem, because I was way more social than ever before. I was also not drinking quite as much as I used to. An accomplishment on two fronts.

Sure, looked at from one narrow-minded perspective, I had failed my sobriety. But examined through another, less fanatical lens, I had made real progress with my people skills.

It seemed therefore reasonable that I should touch base with a therapist. The popularly vague wisdom is that one should choose a therapist based on the recommendation of a trusted friend. But I had no such trusted friend; I had something better: I chose a therapist based on the price of real estate in Manhattan. To me, how bad could a therapist be if he was able to maintain an office along Central Park West with Lauren Bacall and Yoko Ono as neighbors?

That late fall afternoon, Central Park was like a snow globe that had been shaken, except instead of white flakes there were colorful leaves swirling past the lampposts and down along the winding paths. The air was cool and crisp as if imported from Switzerland. Looking up, I saw the shape of Jackie O in a cloud formation; she was wearing an Hermès scarf around her head and carrying a crocodile Kelly bag. She was about to be consumed by a giant panda.

It occurred to me that I had lived in New York City for thirteen years, and yet this was only the third time I had been to Central Park. The other two times were also that week. The first was on Monday when the cabdriver drove through it on the way to my new therapist in a building just down the street from the Dakota (where, as the old New York joke goes, *Rosemary's Baby* and John Lennon were both shot). My second park experience was an hour later in the taxi home.

I paid the fare and stepped out of the cab. A hot dog vendor was at the corner, and I wondered if my shrink got lunch from him. When I got upstairs to his office, I'd see if I could detect faint ketchup stains on the front of his shirt or tie.

I made my way to the building and found the cavernous elevator. When I reached the floor, I arrived at a door with four buzzers, each with an engraved brass nameplate. I pushed the buzzer marked Dr. Howard Schwartz, and after a brief pause, the door unlocked.

The communal waiting area was composed of utilitarian chairs that were comfortable enough for five minutes and a glass-topped coffee table spread with magazines I didn't even realize were still in print, like *Sunset* and *Ladies' Home Journal*. A narrow hallway led away from the waiting area, lined with four white doors, each closed.

Just as I was sitting down and reaching for a *Saturday Evening Post* that could have been—or maybe was—from the

1970s, one of the doors opened, and there was Dr. Schwartz. This was the second time I'd seen him, but I'd forgotten what he looked like. He was so ordinary in appearance—a generic, middle-aged Caucasian mental health professional—that I wondered if anyone ever recognized him anywhere. I thought, *He would make the perfect criminal.*

I nodded and stood, hoping I didn't look insane.

He motioned for me to come into his office.

The ritual of therapy had begun.

His office was completely nondescript, as befitting the man himself. Add a poster of a palm tree and it could have been a travel agency; slide a Texas Instruments calculator onto the desk and he could be an accountant. If there had been a dildo and a video camera in the room, he could even have passed for an ironic pornographer.

It was an utterly conflict-free space.

I sat in the brown leather recliner next to the table with a box of tissues on top, and he sat across from me in the black leather recliner. They were identical chairs in different colors. The patient's was brown, I decided, because he or she had not yet reached the degree of self-awareness to occupy the black.

"So," Dr. Schwartz began, "how were things this week?" He smiled pleasantly, as if we were old friends catching up.

"I think pretty great," I said, smiling back at him. I picked up where we left off in our last session, which was also our first. He knew that I'd relapsed, but I hadn't yet told him how I'd spent Thanksgiving.

I found that I was excited to tell him, mostly because it gave me the chance to talk about Mitch's Famous Author

Friend, and that was the next-best thing to seeing him again. Besides, I was a new patient and therefore determined to be his most entertaining, so of course I was going to name-drop.

Already, Dr. Schwartz was vastly superior to other therapists I had seen over the years because he said things. For example, he admitted that he thought my departure from strict sobriety into delicate moderate drinking was not the rough-and-tumble fall off the wagon some might consider it to be but rather a sign that I was taking control of my life. He was very positive about it, in fact.

Something latent and Baptist within me felt like shouting, "Amen!" It was one of the most liberating and invigorating therapy sessions I'd ever had. Anxiety had paralyzed me before the confession. I hated having to explain my alcoholism and subsequent relapse at the first therapy session, before I'd had enough time to make him like me. It was like being on a first date and letting your worst, awful self ooze out all over the table. That stress and worry had been for nothing, because his reaction was the next-best thing to reaching around behind his chair, grabbing a bottle of Veuve Clicquot, and popping the cork right there—cheers!

I crossed my legs and filled him in on my week. I told him about how Mitch and I spent Thanksgiving, and when I mentioned Famous Author's name, Dr. Schwartz's face lit up.

"Wow, that's impressive," Dr. Schwartz said. "He's a genius. I've read several of his books."

It seemed trivial to mention the fact that the turkey was juicy, but Dr. Schwartz appeared to believe it was significant, because he asked, "You don't happen to know how he prepared the turkey, do you?"

I felt just the smallest pang of failure in my chest that it hadn't even occurred to me to get the recipe. "No, we arrived too late for that," I said.

I felt so at ease, I even described Mitch's spotty body hair and compared it to Famous Author Friend's much more evenly distributed fur. "You could almost comb the hair on his forearms," I said, "while with Mitch, it's more like somebody tried to scrub it off with a scouring pad."

Dr. Schwartz nodded and told me that nutritional deficiencies can result in irregular body hair loss. And furthermore, many psychological illnesses have a nutritional component. He was happy that I was expanding my social circle and didn't spend the holiday locked up alone in my apartment, as I'd admitted doing for years.

I thought, *Yeah, that's a good point.*

As uncomfortable as the subject made me, I felt I had to discuss sex.

Because when I told myself things were perfect with Mitch, I meant they were perfect except for the sex. For some reason, I couldn't seem to get or maintain an erection around Mitch. For the first few weeks, I was able to blame this on our late nights of drinking. But eventually, Mitch began pestering me for a better explanation. The trouble was, I didn't know why my body failed to react the way it should around him.

When I explained this to Dr. Schwartz, he began to frown as he listened and nodded. At one point, he asked if I was able to get erections when I was not around Mitch.

"Oh yeah," I said. "All the time, like a teenager. Sometimes at work for no reason. It's annoying."

He nodded at this, as though it served as some sort of confirmation.

I admitted that I didn't find Mitch appealing when he was not wearing clothes. "He works out, a lot. But only his upper body. His legs are really skinny and pale, and the hair on them is especially thin and weird looking."

Dr. Schwartz told me it wasn't surprising I was experiencing intimacy issues. "He sounds quite imbalanced and negative."

I nodded. "You totally get it."

"And there's not much sexy about a negative attitude."

This seemed incredibly obvious, yet it hadn't occurred to me. I rolled my eyes. "Oh my God, that is so true."

The doctor looked at me pointedly.

"But I really love him," I said. "I want the sex to work."

Dr. Schwartz asked me, "What do you love about Mitch?" He poised his pen above his pad, ready to take copious notes.

I had to think about it for a moment. "Well, he's genuinely peculiar, not, you know, like a poser acting weird. And he's broken, which is sad and appealing, I guess. He's definitely smart. He's hilarious, though I don't think he's trying to be funny or really even knows that he is, so it's accidental."

His advice was, "Sex extends from deep intimacy. You can't rush these things."

Tremendous relief made my body feel instantly lighter. Now Mitch couldn't pester me about the frequency of our sex because a true and proper psychiatrist said so. More importantly, I realized that even though Dr. Schwartz was completely un-hot, I would much rather have sex with him than with Mitch. I didn't say this out loud but only because

I couldn't think of how to phrase it without it sounding like an insult.

Toward the end of the session, Dr. Schwartz told me to pay careful attention to my own thoughts and motivations. He instructed me, "Be as honest with yourself about your feelings as possible. Knowing what you don't feel is also a feeling." He added, "And don't beat yourself up like Mitch does."

We scheduled an appointment for the following week, and I left his office feeling a glimmer of excitement. Part of me felt I was fooling myself. Because part of me believed that an alcoholic can't ever drink again. But the rest of me felt pretty good and would feel even better after a martini.

Mitch went to many parties and out to many dinners during the holiday season, and because I was his shiny new boyfriend, I went too.

The week before Christmas, we went to Moomba, downtown on Sixth Avenue near Christopher Street.

Moomba had no sign, of course; you just had to know. And then they had to let you in. Because it was so new and so "it," normal people couldn't go there. The only reason I was there was because of the guy I was dating and not having sex with.

Mitch was getting angry with Colin, another famous writer who was sitting next to him.

Colin told Mitch, "Did you know 'I fucked my mother' is an anagram of your name? It's true. I figured it out in the green room today."

"You are such an idiot. There's no *F* in my name. What's the matter with you? And I don't like the idea of you sitting around thinking about my name so much; it's disturbing. Just don't think about me." Mitch pointedly angled his body away from Colin.

Colin laughed and gulped his cocktail.

Famous Author Friend had secured a huge table in the center of the room. Goldie Hawn was at the table across from us, and Cindy Crawford was downstairs, near the door.

Mitch pointed her out when we first came in. "She has to stay downstairs here in the common bar area because of that terrible movie she made with Billy Baldwin," he said.

The waiter looked at me with disinterest because I was the only one at our table who was not famous or sitting next to someone famous. Despite this, I managed to catch his attention.

"Can I have another cosmopolitan?" I asked. This would be my fourth.

At the word *cosmopolitan*, the entire table, every head, turned toward the waiter, and all at once, everybody began barking out drink orders, which at first seemed to panic him until he realized everybody was ordering the same thing, cosmos all around.

Martha Stewart stopped by the table and whispered something into Famous Author Friend's ear and made him laugh.

I spent the night with my arm around Mitch, dressed like a good old boy from the South, with my Pabst trucker hat, which I had seen on several other people recently and therefore would have to stop wearing soon. I felt very relaxed and content. I even thought to myself, *Life is kind of wonderful now.*

Later in the evening, though, after I had consumed several more drinks, Mitch and I got into an argument over, of all things, Brita water filters—the kind you screw onto your faucet. Mitch had one and thought it was the most brilliant invention ever. I didn't like it at all because it slowed the water too much.

He took it personally.

"They're not slow. What are you talking about? That's just plain wrong. You're crazy."

I said, "Well, they definitely slow down the flow from the faucet. But I like that they take all the shit out of the water. So I agree, they are pretty great overall. If you have the patience for the trickle."

And that was the word that really sent him off.

He shouted, "Trickle? How can you even say that?" He'd never been mad at me before, but he sure was now.

He was so loud that Famous Author Friend suddenly turned away from whatever other conversation he was having and bore right into our fight. He said, "Are you talking about Brita filters?" His eyes were penetrating and intense. But the corners of his mouth were turned up ever so slightly into the hint of a smile. He looked spectacular.

Mitch kind of coughed and took a belt of his drink, which by this point was a neat scotch. "It's ridiculous. He's saying they slow the water down too much so he doesn't want one, which is nuts and annoying."

The glass in Mitch's hand was actually trembling, he was so upset.

Famous Author Friend said, "Augusten is right, Mitch. Brita filters practically *stop* the water flow."

Then he smiled at me.

And that's when I realized he was the one I wanted to have sex with, not Mitch. But then I immediately told myself, *That's bullshit star-fucking.*

Mitch turned to me and said, "Hey, baby, I'm sorry." He was smiling, but he looked desperate, and this broke my heart a little.

I turned away from Famous Author Friend. "I love you," I said to Mitch, trying to look like I meant it, because I did.

"I know," he said back to me. "I love you, too."

We left Moomba at a little past midnight and went back to Mitch's apartment, where we climbed into bed. We were watching CNN and wearing underwear. A baby was dead because the mother shook it, and now she was in jail. The CNN anchor appeared to be on the verge of tears, personally horrified by the story she was reading off the teleprompter.

Suddenly, Mitch rolled on top of me, grabbed my shoulders, and shook me hard.

"Don't shake the baby. Don't shake the baby," he said, and then he gnashed his teeth and grinned.

I laughed really hard and thought, *This is why I love you. Because you're random and funny and weird.*

He stopped shaking me and looked intently into my eyes. His own eyes appeared gentle and drunk, the eyelids heavy, lashes suddenly moist.

I was not at all expecting it when he lunged forward and began kissing me. But because I didn't see it coming, instead of a kiss, it was more like his open mouth was covering my lips and he was sliding his tongue over them.

My body was fighting with itself because I wanted to

shove him back, wipe my mouth on my arm, and say, "Oh my God, no wonder you were single for so long if that's how you kiss."

But of course I couldn't do that, so I was trying to just breathe through my nose and not freak out.

He reached down, and my dick was soft, which made me think, *Well, yeah.* But he was hard and grinding against my hip bone in a high-pressure spiral. His hot, wet tongue was frantically searching my mouth, looking for fillings. My tongue was crouched so far back in my throat I thought I might actually swallow it.

Finally he raised his head, eyes tightly shut. "Oh God!" he cried. "Jesus fucking Christ!" And he came with a violent tremor against my femur. His body relaxed on top of mine, all his weight on my chest so that I had to take shallow breaths. After a few leaden moments, he rolled off me and fell asleep.

The next morning, Mitch was tense.

His face was etched with fine shadows in the bright morning light. He'd been awake for hours by the time I opened my own eyes at six. His forehead was sweaty.

"We need to talk," he said.

The only thing worse than having "the sex talk" is having it with the sun in my eyes before I've peed and brushed my teeth. "What do we need to talk about?" I asked, even though I already knew.

"Why do you withdraw from me when we make love? I mean, what specifically goes through your mind?" he asked.

I sat up and told him I didn't know. "It's just like something blank, a wall rises up and blocks everything. Or like a coma," I said.

"Having sex with me is like being in a coma?" he said.

I said, "I didn't mean it that way."

The problem was, I just couldn't tell him the actual whole truth, because that would ruin everything.

I thought back to what I told my shrink. "I don't find Mitch sexy. And I keep thinking I will. I'm waiting for that attraction to kick in, but it hasn't. And I can't tell him this, because then it would be over, and that's not what I want."

Finally, Mitch said, "We'll figure it out. I love you."

"We will," I agreed. Then I got dressed and walked the few blocks home to my own studio apartment, where I crawled back into bed.

I couldn't fall asleep, though, because I felt resentful and angry at my own brain. Why should I have to be attracted to Mitch simply to have sex with him? I'd had sex with people who repulsed me before.

It just didn't seem fair.

"It happened again the night before last," I told Dr. Schwartz.

"What happened?" he asked, yellow notepad poised to take notes of my illness and transgressions.

"The not-having-sex thing. It happened again, and it's getting worse. He's talking to me about it. I keep telling him that it's always like this for me, that it takes time. The other morning, he said, 'How much time? It's been three months, and I'm worried.' Everything is so right between us except this."

I liked that first therapy session way more, before we started talking about sex.

"What do you think the reason is?" he asked. "Why are you pulling back from him?"

I was annoyed with Dr. Schwartz for asking the same question Mitch asked me. If I knew the answer, I wouldn't have been sitting in that office in the first place. If I knew the reason, the reason would go away. Like turning on a light to erase a shadow.

"I don't know," I said.

"But you love Mitch, correct?" he asked.

"Yes," I said quickly. "I do. I know I do. He's perfect for me. We are like two pieces of the same puzzle; we fit together. I know that sounds trite, but many true things are."

He considered this. "It doesn't sound trite," he said. "It sounds good. That's what mature love is."

"But shouldn't mature love also involve sex?" I pressed. Had he forgotten what I just told him?

"Yes, sex is a part of a healthy, loving relationship. It's a way to express love for another person. But not the only way."

This struck me as something a person trapped in a sexless marriage would say, as opposed to a psychiatrist. I looked at his hand to see if he was wearing a wedding band, and in fact he was: thin and platinum. I imagined that this last comment was what his wife told him sex is like for her.

"Please, darling, stop. There are other ways for us to express our love. Would you hand me my book?"

I imagined him looking at amateur porn on the Internet and jerking off into a Kleenex while his wife read a novel in the other room.

"Are you okay?" he asked me.

"I'm fine. I just spaced out," I lied.

"Did you experience another disassociation?" That was the first time he had labeled what it was that I did, the temporary coma thing.

"Yes, I went blank. I go blank when I think about sex with Mitch. I need to fix this. I don't want to fuck up the relationship."

He looked at the clock behind me. "Well, we have to close for today," he said. He reached down on the floor for his appointment book, which was leaning against the base of his chair. "Friday, same time?" he asked.

"Fine," I said, but as I left his office, I felt irritated not to be fixed already.

In the cab, it occurred to me that Dr. Schwartz would look gross naked; smooth and kind of gray, like a dolphin. Why couldn't I practice having sex with him, right there in a clinical setting? Afterward, he could show me how to transfer it all over to Mitch.

Even though I didn't think mine was a "sex is currency" issue like some people have, sex really was a form of currency, and a universal one at that. Occasionally, it was the only way to get someone to shut the fuck up and stay with you.

In the dream, we're in a Jeep—I think it's green. I'm the passenger; he's the driver. I've never seen him before; he's not somebody I know in the waking world, but here, I do. Jeep Guy is driving up a nearly vertical trail somewhere in the Rocky Mountains. The canvas top is down, and the doors are off. Though normally I would rather serve time in a federal prison than in nature, I am totally at ease and filled with the sensation of wanting nothing more.

This is not a feeling I have in my non-dreaming life. I always want something else.

The sun is incredibly bright and hot because we're so close to it.

I glance over at his strong, handsome face, which has a weathered ruggedness about it, like he's been on this trail many times before. He has thick, straight blond hair that's swept up and back. I have never dated a guy with blond hair, though I am aware of a sense of inevitability. Like, of course he's a rugged blond dude.

I also feel lucky. I have a sense that he's more handsome and robust and capable than anyone I have ever known. Appropriate (for me) thoughts like *Where the fuck are the doors!?* or *A mountain lion could just leap right in here at any moment!* are not of concern. I am not thinking about the lack of airbags, the steep drop on my side of the trail, rattlesnakes, skin cancer, brake failure, or dehydration.

We're not talking, but I'm not paranoid about what he's thinking. *Does he hate my hair?* is not in the front of my mind like usual. There is nothing to add or subtract, nothing to change or wish for. I am just exactly and perfectly fine.

Then I woke up, and my heart beat a couple of extra times with the shock of suddenly being transported from the Rocky Mountains with my ruggedly handsome blond Jeep Guy to my pathetic studio apartment on Third Avenue in

Manhattan with one dirty window overlooking the ass end of a bunch of other apartment buildings.

And I was crushed.

It was the worst tumble-to-earth sensation, the harshest of rude awakenings I'd ever had. And unlike normal dreams, it didn't evaporate around the edges as soon as I awoke. It remained fixed in my mind, like a memory.

I showered and wondered, *Who is he?* I thought about telling Mitch over dinner, because it would give us something new to talk about instead of the state of his writing career. But then I realized, I can't tell Mitch, because he can't compare with Jeep Guy, and he would see this in my eyes.

It was spring. Mitch and I were having medium-rare steaks with a peppery crust and dry martinis at the Old Homestead restaurant in the meat-packing district, sitting in a deep-red leather booth and talking about sex.

When he asked if there was something different I would like to do in bed, he raised his eyebrows, and I knew he was trying to ascertain if I had a secret fetish I'd been too shy to confess. Like, if only he would wear a giant raccoon-fur suit, then I could get it up. It was both touching and annoying, and I was tempted to tell him the truth: "What I would really like to do in bed is be a girl so I could just lie back and fake it."

When this line of questioning led nowhere, Mitch finally told me, "I spoke with Morgan about us."

"You told Morgan?" I said, at once excited and horrified

that his friend, the star of a top-rated prime-time TV show, now knew I was unable to get or maintain an erection in the presence of my boyfriend, who also happened to be my favorite author.

"It was a really good talk. I felt much better," he said as he chewed a french fry down to a stub and then popped it into his mouth.

I felt relieved, as if I had been acquitted.

"What did she say?" I asked, extremely interested because my future now seemed dependent upon the prime-time television star's words.

Mitch balanced his knife on the rim of his plate and looked across the table into my eyes. "She was sexually abused as a child. She told me that when she and Steve first started dating, she couldn't sleep with him. It took her six months."

I wanted to call Morgan, I thought. I wanted to tell an actress about my problems instead of telling the therapist. I wanted Golden Globe advice.

"Everything's fine now between them," Mitch told me.

"That's good, yeah. It really is just a matter of time. I'm just fucked up sexually," I said, offering no depth or insight into the conversation, which actually seemed perfectly acceptable to him, because he smiled and picked up his knife.

The waiter asked us if everything was all right and appeared surprised when we ordered more drinks, as he had just served us two fresh martinis moments ago and now only two sweaty, empty glasses remained.

We didn't say anything for a while. It was not the silence of two people who are so comfortable with each other that they don't need to clutter up their ease with words. It was two people who are quiet because they are concentrating so hard on believing that everything is okay.

Mitch was negative, but he wasn't cynical, somehow. He contained a purity of character, and maybe this was the thing I admired most about him. He had retained a toddler's good nature, but it had been molested by an old man's bitterness. Yet this wasn't really the problem. I can get into bitter old men. I was extremely confused. I found his darkness alluring on the one hand, but maybe I didn't find it sexy?

Later, back at his place, Mitch was lounging on his nubby plaid sofa, and I was kneeling on the rug giving him a blow job. I was thinking, *I'm gay, so this is supposed to be fun.*

I wondered if I should talk to my married therapist about how much work it was to give somebody a blow job and how I really didn't think I liked it at all and what did that mean? As I wondered this, Mitch pulled his dick out of my mouth and finished himself off.

I felt more relief than if I had come, too.

"You didn't have to do that," he said. As if I had scrubbed his kitchen floor with Murphy's Oil Soap.

"I love doing it," I said. Then I stood up and sat next to him on the couch, looking at the wet spots on his T-shirt.

"I need to change out of this shirt," he said, standing up.

Alone on the sofa, the relief I felt was now being replaced by a sucking sense of unnamed dread.

When he returned wearing a fresh T-shirt, he sat at the end of the sofa and turned to face me. "You did that to please me, I know you did. And I know you didn't enjoy it, and it scares me."

I wanted to smack him. The whole point of the blow job was so that we would not have this very conversation. "I'm getting more comfortable, I really am," I told him. Then I thought, *So will you please shut the hell up?*

Mitch looked increasingly agitated. "I feel rejected that I can't make you happy in that way, that I don't turn you on."

On his face was the exact same expression he had when he talked about how Little, Brown turned down his novel.

I stared at the dark television set, and then he looked away from me and stared at the TV, as well. It was as if we were willing it to come on by itself, as if we were waiting for something—anything—to happen.

He left the couch and climbed into bed, which was just a futon on his floor. In less than a minute, he was asleep.

I was wired now from having had all those martinis at dinner followed by the frustrating oral sex and then the messy discussion that followed it. The thought of sitting quietly on his sofa watching the TV on mute or reading a book was unbearable.

So I quietly snuck out the door and walked the three blocks home. It was handy that we lived so close to each other.

I had several more drinks in my apartment, enough to put me in a rowdy mood. Enough to make me pick up my phone.

———

I called an ex-boyfriend who worked as a bartender in Soho and asked if he wanted to get together when he was done for the night.

An hour later, we were crammed against each other in the bathtub of his East Village apartment. We'd just had sex, but it seemed we were about to get at it again.

Sex with Doug had always been excellent. It was everything else between us that didn't work. Nothing that came out of his mouth interested me in the slightest. And his ears seemed to turn off whenever I spoke a word.

It was almost six in the morning when I finally dressed and walked back home to my place. Once there, I sat on my bed in the dim, opening light of the morning and thought, *Now it's over with Mitch. Now that I've cheated on him, I can't ever be honest.*

I lay back against the pillows and stared up at the ceiling. I hated myself. I thought, *I am just a destructive force in the world. Look at all the bodies I leave behind me.*

By the close of the following week, I had decided not to tell Mitch about my infidelity because I'd come to see it in a different light. I hadn't simply been horny and called an ex to get off. It had been far more academic in nature: I needed to see if I even could still have sex.

Which I could.

So I had learned that nothing was broken exactly.

The problem was that sex with an ex-boyfriend isn't ideal from a research point of view. There was history, familiarity, a certain degree of comfort and ease. That one night, I realized, simply hadn't told me enough. It would be far more helpful to observe my emotions and responses with somebody I didn't know. A stranger. Therapy could take forever to fix a complex sexual issue like mine. What if I could fix it myself? Wasn't it worth a try at least?

Especially considering Mitch's latest ultimatum. He'd confronted me early one morning with another frank discussion about the withered state of our sexual relationship. Very soon, he said, we needed to resolve the sexual issues between us, because he was feeling increasingly frustrated and hurt. "It's making me want to cheat on you," he told me. "And that makes me hate myself even more than I already do."

He further admitted that Famous Author Friend "thinks we should break up. He said if we're not having sex, we don't have a real relationship, anyway."

I was horrified that Mitch had talked about this stuff with him. Because now, a gigantic stopwatch had been set above my head. If I didn't fix myself fast, Mitch would have no choice but to dump me. Then at next year's holiday parties, I would be talked about as the unsexual ex-boyfriend, the one with a smooth, Ken-doll crotch.

What bothered me most of all was that I had been neutered in the eyes of Famous Author Friend himself.

And that would simply not do.

The ticking of the stopwatch above my head—*get fixed, have sex, get fixed, have sex*—placed me in a constant state of anxiety.

I thought of sex incessantly. Not of having it but of why I wasn't. When I closed my eyes to sneeze, I saw Mitch's pale, skinny legs, his wiggling toes. I heard, "Hey, baby!" spoken in a goofy, cartoonish voice.

If he wasn't sullen and depressed, Mitch was playful and odd. He collected action figures and wore superhero underwear. His rumpled hair made him look like Bart Simpson's older brother.

I was pretty goofy, too. In many ways, it seemed, we were so much alike. And this was what made me pause and wonder, exactly *how much* alike?

On AOL, you could have up to five different screen names, each with a different profile. Mitch's profile, attached to the only screen name I knew, contained several unusual abbreviations.

Brn for his hair, *Bloo* to describe his eye color. His height and weight were not approximate but exact, because Mitch was obsessive about his body, though only the top half.

He listed the circumference of his chest: fifty-three inches.

AOL allowed you to search member profiles by entering information into any of the search fields. You could search by age, astrological sign; whatever string of characters you entered would be matched against existing member profiles.

The results were returned in the form of a list.

When I did this, it spat back two names: one was Mitch's own e-mail address, the one I used every day.

And a second, unfamiliar screen name: RealGuy100.

I clicked on the link to open the profile, and almost line for line, it was a match with Mitch's, except that this screen name listed him as single as opposed to blank like his familiar profile. Blank, of course, could mean many things, one of which was "seriously dating somebody and madly in love."

I knew two things: this was *definitely* Mitch, and single meant *single*.

I immediately added RealGuy100 to my buddy list. The next time he logged on, his name would appear in a little window on the corner of my screen, along with the names of other people I knew who were also online.

I waited.

A half hour later, RealGuy100's name popped up.

AOL allowed you to click a name, and if the person was in a public chat room, it would tell you which one. I pressed the LOCATE MEMBER ONLINE button and it said, "RealGuy100 is in member chat room NewYorkCity Men 4 Men NOW."

I thought, *Well, well, well.*

I poured myself a tall glass of scotch and settled in. This was deeply thrilling.

How far would he go? Would he actually hook up with somebody? Would he have sex with some complete stranger and then act as if nothing had happened the next time we were together?

Obviously, I realized, I had no choice. If Mitch was sneaking around behind my back and having sex with people he met in common chat rooms, that would change everything. I could never be with somebody who wasn't trustworthy and monogamous.

I would have to lay a trap.

I created my own new screen name: SwellGuyNY. I added a fantasy profile, assembling all the physical qualities I knew Mitch found attractive in a man. When SwellGuyNY entered the same chat room and Mitch clicked on the screen name, the profile would be irresistible to him.

Using his own profile measurements as a starting point, I subtracted one inch in height and added several inches to the diameter of my legs. I then named several movies, all of which I knew to be Mitch's favorites. I quoted something from a book I knew he loved and said I had a dog, because one of Mitch's greatest sources of complaint was that his building would not allow them and someday he wanted one.

I logged on under my new name and clicked my way into the chat room where I'd seen RealGuy100. There were twenty-three other people in the room. Instantly, a chat window appeared with RealGuy100's name.

What's up?

Thinking of hooking up, I replied.

Me too, he said.

I asked, *What are you into?*

He wrote, *Totally versatile . . . love kissing . . . getting really oral, etc.*

It was the *etc.* that made me feel queasy. What the fuck did that mean? I could not believe that I was dating somebody who would "etc." with strangers and then wanted to kiss me with that same RealGuy100 mouth.

I now loathed Mitch. I typed, *Send me your picture?*

He did, and it was Mitch, a scan of his six-year-old author photo. His mother had taken the picture.

I logged off. I just dumped him there. Now, not only was his boyfriend rejecting him sexually at home but so were the guys in the AOL chat room. Perhaps this new anonymous rejection would send him into a spiral of misery, which I felt he absolutely deserved.

An hour later, he called and left a message on my answering machine. "Are we getting together later?" he asked.

I didn't call him back. He called three more times, and I let the machine answer.

The following morning when he called, I did pick up. "Hey," I said, upbeat.

He was crying. "What did I do? Are you mad at me? Where have you been?"

I told him I'd been exhausted and fallen asleep last night.

He said he was going crazy because it felt like things between us were falling apart. He asked if I'd been to my psychiatrist, and I told him, "He bumped me up to twice a week."

Then I suggested we take some *space*.

I used exactly that word because it's the most infuriating word of all.

He tearfully muttered, "Maybe space is a good thing."

Of course, it never is, but he agreed. He was sniffling when he hung up.

A minute later, RealGuy100 logged on and went into a chat room. I'd cloaked my name, made myself invisible so he couldn't see me but I could see him. Now I knew that my sexually frustrated and weepy boyfriend was completely willing to screw around on me behind my back.

And I knew this because I was stalking him like a psychopath online. I was exactly like Kathy Bates in *Misery*, except not as fat and therefore more nimble.

Dr. Schwartz looked drained that evening when I arrived for my emergency appointment at eight. A puffy-faced, red-eyed woman who had obviously been crying for the last fifty minutes was just leaving his office when I got there, and he ushered me in immediately. No doubt she had originally been his last appointment for the day, so I actually felt sorry for him.

But once I pulled out all my printouts, the pages and pages of documentation detailing Mitch's online exploits with strangers, each of which happened to be me using a different screen name, Dr. Schwartz seemed anything but weary.

Each of my different online identities had a unique photo, lifted from elsewhere on the Web. Along with this, I had brought a stack of e-mails from Mitch, with lines like "I would never cheat on you, but maybe we have to have an open relationship even though that's not what I want."

Using these documents, I explained what I had done, or rather, how I'd tried to fix myself.

He was riveted.

He was holding all my printouts in his lap. "Help me understand," he said. "After you had bathtub sex with your ex-boyfriend, what triggered the series of affairs that followed?"

I explained how the first affair happened because I thought maybe I needed to "practice." Maybe I just needed to oil the machinery and I would be okay. I could forgive myself, I thought, because I was doing it for us, not me.

"Besides," I explained, "with an ex-boyfriend, it's easy to just sort of add that one sexual encounter to all the other times you had sex before, when you were a couple. So in a real sense, that first affair didn't even happen."

Dr. Schwartz nodded. He was following me. Possibly, he even approved of my logic. It was hard to know for sure.

"The next affair happened because the first one really didn't teach me anything, and I thought, *I have to do this again but with a total stranger.* But that was a failure, as well, because the guy I had sex with was physically much more my type than Mitch."

"I'm confused," he said. "How was this second affair a failure? Were you unable to get an erection?"

"No," I explained. "I got several erections. It was a failure because the guy was much hotter than Mitch could ever be. So it wasn't a fair and unbiased study, you know what I mean? It's like, obviously, I can get it up for the Brazilian soccer player with the philosophy scholarship at NYU, because who wouldn't be able to get it up for him? I mean, he was semipro, you know?"

Dr. Schwartz glanced up at the ceiling as if performing calculations. Eventually, he looked back at me and said, "Okay, I think I've got it straight."

I continued. "The third affair happened because I couldn't tell after either of the first two whether this was a control issue I was dealing with or maybe the need to be degraded. I just didn't know. So I picked a guy who was just plain ugly, and we went back to his place in Brooklyn. Everything about him was tacky, including his apartment. I mean, he was really nobody's type."

"And?" Dr. Schwartz asked, leaning forward with what I thought might perhaps be an extra degree of interest.

"And I couldn't really get it up at first. Only when I pretended I was a hustler, then I could. That's when I knew it wasn't about being degraded. It was about control. But control of what?"

He shook his head like he just didn't know.

"Exactly," I said. "That's why the fourth affair had to happen. I had to find out what it was I was trying to control."

"So, what was this fourth affair?" he asked.

I leaned back against the brown leather and looked at him with importance. "It was the fourth affair that told me everything," I said.

Dr. Schwartz leaned so far forward he was in real danger of tipping his chair off balance and tumbling onto the carpet. "And why is that?"

"Because the fourth affair was with George," I admitted.

"Who's George?" Dr. Schwartz asked, puzzled. He began riffling through his notes. "I don't recall that name. Have you mentioned him?"

I sighed and looked down at the arm of the chair. "No, I don't think I've mentioned George yet. But probably, I should have," I said.

George had been one of the first people I met after moving to Manhattan in 1989. He was an investment banker, and on our first date, I learned two stunning things about him. First, his office was directly across the street from my Battery Park City apartment. In fact, from his desk, he would be able to peer out the window and look directly into my bedroom. The other thing I learned was that he had a "roommate," which made no sense to me because he was an investment banker and thus shouldn't need a roommate.

This was actually the last thing he told me on our date after he handed me his phone number: "And if somebody else answers, don't worry; it's just my roommate."

As I walked away, I actually considered tossing the number into the trash because, *roommate, my ass*. But then? It spooked me that he could see my apartment from his office. Because nobody lived downtown in my neighborhood. It was originally created from the landfill generated during the construction of the Twin Towers, so New Yorkers jeered at the neighborhood. It was considered the New Jersey of Manhattan. The fact that George could see my unmade bed from his desk drenched our meeting in destiny.

As I sat in the windowsill of my apartment overlooking the West Side Highway, I held the scrawled number in my hand. Somehow I knew that to call it would alter my life.

Of course, I had been right. There had never been a roommate, only a lover of almost seven years who was dying of AIDS. The lover had contracted the virus by having an affair. George remained HIV negative.

I fell in love with him. And one of the things I loved most about him was that he wouldn't leave his boyfriend for me. They'd been out of love for several years, but George couldn't abandon him. This made him mythic in my mind. Heroic.

I was absolutely obsessed with him. Because I couldn't see him constantly and we had to meet downtown at my apartment during lunch or at night when he was walking his dog, I redecorated my apartment to look like his.

Then his boyfriend became seriously sick and was hospitalized. There was a great deal of bleeding, and George couldn't bring himself to wear gloves. Several months later, the boyfriend was dead, and George tested positive himself.

And suddenly, he was mine. Everything I wanted, I had. Except I knew I couldn't really have it.

He'd been HIV positive now for five years. And all this time, I'd been trying my hardest to fall out of love with him.

"I don't understand," Dr. Schwartz interjected. "Why have you spent so much time trying not to be in love with George?"

I just looked at him as though he were a madman. "Because George is dying," I said. "I mean, he wasn't dying at first, but I knew he would eventually, and now he is. And why on earth would I want to be with somebody who was only going to abandon me?"

Now Dr. Schwartz leaned back in his chair and resumed the more traditional posture of a psychotherapist. "I see," he said.

"So I've been pulling away from him, you know? Especially over the last two years, I've really pulled back. And he's become sicker and sicker. Over the past six months, I've hardly seen him at all. And when I have, it's been shocking."

An image of George waiting for me on a bench outside

a coffee place on Hudson Street came to mind. He was so skinny. He had a walking cane leaning against his knee.

I went on. "I just felt like if I could make him fade away instead of just suddenly vanishing right in the middle of love, that would be easier, you know?"

To my enormous surprise, my eyes flooded with tears.

"Has it worked?" Dr. Schwartz asked.

Well, that's not fair, I thought. *You can't ask that question after you see the tears.*

"No," I said. "I mean, yes," I corrected myself. "It has worked. In a way. I mean, I'm not in love with him anymore. I'm in love with Mitch instead."

He nodded but didn't say anything, so I went on.

"It's just that, well, I wondered something. I wondered if I could still have sex with George, after all this time. It's been almost a year. And sex with him was the best sex I ever had. It always had been."

"Is that right?" Dr. Schwartz asked.

He looked sad, and I wondered if he was just so tired of hearing people's problems all day. I wondered if he'd rather be home watching game shows and eating takeout lasagna from Zabar's.

"So I called him up, and he was totally shocked to hear from me, but he was also really happy. I asked if I could come over, and he said, 'Yes, right away, come now.'"

Dr. Schwartz leaned over and plucked a tissue from the iris-printed box, and I expected him to hand it to me and was about to thank him, but he kept it for himself. He just held on to it, resting his hands on top of my computer printouts in his lap.

A strange feeling of loss began to creep over me as I kept talking. "So I went over to George's apartment and had sex with him. Even though he's wasted away to nothing and was hooked up to an IV line and even though it was the most awful, sickening scene in some horrible way? It was also the best sex I've ever had. Even though the only thing that happened was he rubbed my dick through my jeans. He didn't even rub it, he just put his hand on top of my lap as we sat side by side on the edge of his bed, and I came instantly, harder than I've ever come in my life."

Somehow, Dr. Schwartz seemed to know in advance what I was going to say, because he already had the most sorrowful expression on his face.

I told him the rest. And that's when I understood why the sex has been so fucked up with Mitch.

Dr. Schwartz blinked, and it was one of those blinks where your eyes don't open back up right away. And when he finally did open them, it was like there was something new and awful there in his glance. Not a judgment, really, but more like a reflection.

"We didn't say anything. We just sat there on the sofa, and I understood everything. The problem is, I really am monogamous. You know? I've spent the last two years trying not to love somebody who's dying, but it didn't work. I just didn't know that until . . . until I did know. And now I can't *not* know it. And when George walked me to the door, it took five minutes because he can barely stand now. When I hugged him good-bye, I felt like I had come home. Only there had been a fire, so everything I was hugging was crumbling in my arms because home was almost not there anymore. I was too late."

The leather squeaked as he uncrossed his legs and placed the papers on the floor at his feet. He propped his elbows on his knees and asked me, "What were you too late for, Augusten?"

I looked into his eyes, and then my gaze shifted to the clock behind his head. It was now almost nine forty-five. But he hadn't even noticed.

I'm the one who said, "I think we ran over."

When your psychiatrist forgets to look at the clock and is hanging on your every word, that's when you know, out of all his patients, you are the sickest.

He ignored my remark and said it again. "What were you too late for, Augusten?"

And I said, "I was too late for everything."

"What's everything?" he asked me.

I said, "Everything is George. He's everything. He's the only thing. He's always been the only thing. I've tried to make him smaller, but it didn't work. And if you could have seen him, oh my God, you would know. There isn't any time left at all."

He sat up straight and said, "That's where you're wrong, my friend."

I liked that he called me *friend*.

"You have more time than you realize. And I'm afraid, very soon, you may see this for yourself."

———

The cab ride home was exhilarating and also like being in a coffin. It seemed the headlights were suddenly turned on, just in time to see the approaching cliff.

I had to confess all that I had done to Mitch. The relationship was over; this would kill it. It was dying, but this would shoot it in the head and put it out of its misery. My first thought was to stand outside his building so that when he got home from work at seven, he'd see me.

Then I realized I should just tell him on the phone. That way, he could hang up on me and be done with me sooner. It would make me look like a coward, but given what I did and how insanely unforgivable it all was, it seemed worth it to be a coward when it spared him from having to walk out of a restaurant or tell me to leave and then slam the door behind me.

So I called him.

But his machine answered, so I hung up. I called again a half hour later. And then I kept calling every fifteen minutes.

At this point, I kind of freaked myself out, because I was calling and calling and calling and calling and calling, leaving all these hang-ups on his machine, all so I could tell him, "Hey, so, I've been stalking you on AOL, and I know you've been trying to hook up with other guys, because I've been posing as those other guys. I also cheated on you four times, but that doesn't really count, because it was self-help."

By ten, I'd stopped trying to reach him, because where the fuck was he? The cyclone of madness in my head had spun all the way around, and now, at this late hour, everything seemed to be entirely his fault.

I even toyed with the idea of not telling him I'd been stalking him or that I'd cheated. I could make plans to meet him—under a false AOL identity—at a certain time and place. Then I, as myself, would happen to walk by and see him waiting, where I would "suddenly" put two and two together—"You're cheating on me, oh my God!"—and break up with him on the spot, saving face.

But he called me at eleven. I'd totally forgotten he was going to a party with Famous Author Friend, even though he'd been talking about it all week. He sounded pretty shit faced, but he wanted to come over, anyway.

"I don't think that's such a good idea," I said.

"Well, why not?" he asked worriedly.

It didn't seem like anywhere near the right time to tell him. On the other hand, maybe the alcohol would act as an anesthetic. Combined with being told over the phone, I felt like I was doing all I could to provide five-point seat belts and an airbag.

That's when I realized this was the perfect time. "So, I've been involved in a research project," I began. "And it's time for you to know about it."

Mitch didn't hang up on me like I expected. He adopted an eerie monotone and said, "I just don't know what's best for me. I need some time to think."

I suppose it's fair to say he was aghast at what I'd done. But I also had the impression that he was flattered I'd gone to so much trouble, and he even seemed impressed with how I'd located his other secret online name.

He did say, "Obviously, we're over as a couple. But maybe we can be friends. I don't know."

I felt a helium lift. I hadn't even considered a friendship. I wasn't sure I actually knew what a friendship was. To me, friends were people your boyfriend knew that you went to dinner with sometimes.

We hung up.

I stared at the scuff-marked wall for a minute, thinking about how things with Mitch had been doomed from the start. I had already been in love with somebody who was dying, and soon the day would arrive when the payment would be due. I had believed I could evenly distribute the weight of my loss. Instead, what was going to happen was it would crash into me in one lump sum.

There was nothing I could do except say things to myself like "Whatever's meant to happen will happen." But that didn't change the fact that I may very well have altered the way things were supposed to turn out.

I was on Eighth Avenue at Fourteenth Street, bending over to tie my shoe when a lengthy shadow appeared directly over my hands and the knot I was trying to tie.

There were now white sneakers, jeans, and a pair of legs beside me.

"Who bends over in the middle of the gayest sidewalk in the world and sticks his ass in the air like a baboon?"

It was Mitch, backlit by the sun. He had a mass of shoulder-length hair that the wind was whipping madly around his face.

I was stunned, because how could his short, choppy, reddish-brown sitcom hair grow that long and in just a month or two?

Which was when I realized I hadn't seen him for a year. We'd called each other regularly, but I never imagined he could change physically.

I said, "Wow. Your hair. It looks great."

He turned his head to the side so the wind would blow his hair smooth against the side of his face. "I don't know," he said uncomfortably.

"No, it's good," I lied, because it looked absolutely horrible.

He wasn't sure. "I either want to grow it longer or cut it short again. You really like it?"

"Not really," I said.

"I'm gonna chop it all off as soon as I get home," he said.

I knew he meant this literally. I was used to seeing him standing in front of the mirror and hacking away at his hair with a pair of kitchen scissors. When he was done, he'd grin goofily and say, "See, looks like I paid three hundred bucks for it."

We walked east along Fourteenth Street so we could cut south on University.

He said, "What's bad about my hair? It's not girly, is it?"

Mitch was very circular in his thinking and once on a subject would not let go of it unless you could manage to throw a bone in the other direction.

I asked, "So, have you been working on your book?"

"Well, um. Ah. Sort of," he said.

Mitch had a new science fiction novel coming out the following year, but he was certain it would be a failure.

At least once a week, he talked dramatically about killing himself. He'd say, "I'm really gonna do it." He had said the exact same thing to me when we were boyfriends. He might detail a new method he'd discovered or invented. His latest was to wait for winter, take sleeping pills, and then go to the roof of his apartment building and lie down naked next to the boxwood planters and freeze to death. He said it would be painless.

"Yeah," I said, "and your dick will shrink up, and everybody will assume it was always small." That actually gave him pause.

Over the past year that we'd become e-mail pen pals if not exactly friends, I was mystified that I ever dated him in the first place. I liked him much more than I did when I was in love with him. But it was also obvious that the lack of sexual chemistry on my part was my sanity desperately trying to reach me.

"So, working on a new book?" I asked.

We walked past Newsbar.

Mitch said, "I'm not going to fall for one of your tricks. I know you. You're just trying to make me stop talking about the hair thing. But I'm not going to until you tell me why it's bad."

"It's just, you know. It makes you look a little like a strung-out lesbian park ranger who drinks too much in her trailer."

He stopped. "That is a much more horrible thing for you

to say than all your affairs and *Fatal Attraction* stalking ever was." But he peered at his reflection in the window of the liquor store where he stood. "Maybe," he said, "you're a little bit right."

I walked him back to his place, and along the way, he told me that Famous Author Friend was dating a Prada model whose parents called him and told him to stay away from their son.

"You guys hanging out tonight?" I asked.

He said no. Prada Model was in town doing a shoot for a billboard on Times Square. Then he said, "I have no life. I don't even know why I bother with anything."

"So, what about tonight? Are you going out trolling?"

"I don't go out trolling," he said, running his fingers back through his lesbian park ranger hair.

Except he did go out trolling, because he called me from the bars all the time. "Stop lying. You go to all those seedy places—Dick's, Dicks and Ass, Dick and Ass and Pecs. You make out with your drug dealer in the bathroom at Boiler Room. You called me from a stall," I reminded him.

"I did that once!" he cried, genuinely annoyed and defensive.

I rolled my eyes. "Once that you've admitted. Last week, you let some redheaded stand-up comic rub your crotch at Dick's. You sent me a picture of him, remember?"

"It wasn't Dick's, it was Splash, and that was three weeks ago, and it was just about sex. And he didn't rub my crotch. We just fooled around a little. Kissed is all."

"Yeah, right," I said.

"I don't want to talk to you anymore."

We arrived at his front door.

"Fine," I said. "Go eat your Chickenator."

Mitch was very finicky with his dinner if he was ordering in. He only ordered the Chickenator sandwich from Boots and Saddle, the parmesan hero from the pizza place around the corner, chicken burrito from the filthy Mexican dive, or a cheeseburger with fries, of which he would only eat three.

I am exactly as limited in the foods I eat, except I eat all the fries.

He hugged me good-bye, and it was a surprisingly deep, fast hug.

I headed home but then decided that I wanted to walk. So I passed my building and went farther south, beyond Astor Place and into the Bowery. Here, I landed on the most curious crescent of a street that hugged a park where there was a columned space set with benches. Old Chinese men were playing cards and smoking, and there were several dogs, all with fur that had been petted smooth over many years. I had arrived at a place I'd never seen before, where every detail was entirely unfamiliar.

I stopped walking and watched the old men play cards. I had the feeling I would never be able to find this spot again no matter how tirelessly I tried.

At home, I received the call I had known would arrive. George had died. I had expected to feel relief, but instead I felt, *That's impossible. I require him.*

II

W hen George died, I could not conjure an image of
my life, next week, without him. So I lay on my
bed, and I stayed there, waiting to die. I only got up to buy
scotch, two bottles at a time.

I can say this with authority: a queen-sized mattress can
hold a year's worth of urine and still be perfectly serviceable.

When I drunkenly opened my eyes at half past four in the
afternoon one day, I realized I had entered the week following his death. That life I could not imagine was here, and I
was in it, alive. What had been an impossible future was me,
now, sluggishly, heavily awakening and squinting without
my glasses to see if I could gauge how much scotch remained
in my second bottle on the counter next to the stove.

It was an act of willpower to swing my legs over and
stand. In six clumsy steps, I was across the room and beside
the stove; such was the beauty of a minuscule Manhattan

studio apartment. The bottle of scotch had less than two inches at the bottom. And I hated myself for not being a better planner and buying them four at a time or even six.

I was always so fucking obsessed with what other people thought. Carrying two bottles up to the cashier said, "I'm on my way to a party." Carrying four said, "I'm on my way down."

I would have to brush my teeth and put on clothes and leave my fetid, debris-engorged apartment and then walk across Ninth Street to the liquor store on University Place. (The one near Astor Place was closer, but I'd gone there last night.) Once I accomplished this, I would be able to return to my stomach-contents of a home and be alone again with whatever vapors remained of George. Maybe drunk, I could find a way to be with him again, even if only through the rereading of his e-mails.

It was like being famished and knowing that only the box from the frozen dinner remained, the picture of the meal and not the meal itself. I could lick the glossy cardboard.

So I dressed myself in never-washed jeans and a T-shirt, and on the way to the liquor store, I recognized somebody on the sidewalk that I knew from the Perry Street AA meetings.

I turned away from her because this made me invisible.

I got my two bottles of scotch and returned home.

Nothing happened except I drank the liquor and pissed in the bed, and then I did this 547 more times.

Downing bottle after bottle of scotch was not my only addict behavior during that time. I also consumed enormous quantities of QVC, television's number-one home shopping network. I had witnessed home shopping before. Late at night in that last, desperate attempt to find something watchable among the two hundred channels before going to sleep, I'd paused and gawked in bemused disbelief as an electric egg scrambler was offered forth like a holy grail. But one night, I was just about to scroll past it during prime time when I was stopped by a close-up of a sparkly ring on a small turntable, throwing off color and dazzling brightness as the studio lights hit the facets. I've loved shiny things since childhood, so I watched hungrily as a blond hostess displayed a ruler for the camera and measured the diameter of a ring. Then she measured the profile. I unmuted the sound. "We're talking nearly three carats of Diamonique. And that's a lot of stone presence."

Hours passed, and new hosts appeared looking fresh and knowledgeable. Days passed, and still they offered bangle bracelets and Crock-Pots, plug-in rodent repellents, and cotton wick-crotch panties. Once, I watched for two days straight during a Joan Rivers Classic Collection marathon. But ultimately, the products—even the jewels—were not why I continued to watch it obsessively. I was hooked because it was live television. And they took calls.

People phoned in and spoke to the hosts on air. They talked about how long they had been looking for a green plastic revolving earring tree *just like that one.* And how much weight they had lost using the George Foreman Lean Mean Grilling Machine. Sometimes they called instead of cutting their wrists. Once while I was watching, the cheerful host told a despondent caller, "Please stay on the line.

Our producer will give you the name of an outreach program in your area."

I got goose bumps.

Another time, I was watching while they were presenting a fountain pen. An attractive model was wearing a night-gown and sitting at a desk. She wore a pleasant expression, as if writing the words "forever . . . dreamily . . . longingly . . ." to a distant lover. But when they cut to a shot looking over the model's shoulder, I saw that she had actually written, "By the time you read this note, I'll be gone. Don't come searching for me . . ."

When they cut back to the host, he was repressing a smile. He'd seen the studio monitor. *Those models*, he might have thought. *Always up to some hijinks.*

That's what was so fascinating about home shopping channels. When a sitcom actress slipped and fell on her bony ass, she was landing on an *X* of masking tape that a gaffer placed on the floor of the set. But when one of the hosts dropped her newborn and the baby started to howl, I knew *it was really happening.*

I got a certain rush from QVC. At that pre-Twitter moment in time, it was the purest form of distilled American culture available. It was intravenous marketing. No memorable jingles, no catchy slogans, no playful typography on the screen. Just the pharmaceutical-grade cocaine equivalent of sales, and I was stunned by its purity. Of course, like any drug, it made me do things I would not normally do.

The night before, I hazily recalled, I had purchased $300 worth of gigantic nonskid rug pads . . . despite the fact that my studio apartment was minuscule and already had its own rug of filth. I had been so swept up in the drama of the presentation that I was unable to contain myself, like someone who is admiring the pretty fish swimming near the coral reef and then gets swept away in an undertow. I called the number on the screen and ordered.

"What size?" the operator asked.

"What size do you have?" I was almost shaking with anticipation.

"We have three sizes, sir. Five by seven, six by—"

"Send me all three," I slurred.

The next morning, I woke up and padded across the mashed-flat food container–carpeted floor to sit at my computer, where, without planning to, I opened a blank document and wrote, "You exposed your penis on national television, Max. What am I supposed to do?"

As I wrote these words, I could see in my mind a blond shopping channel host sitting uncomfortably across from his executive producer. There was one of those golf-putting gizmos on the floor, the kind from the in-flight magazine ads. I knew the show host had been wearing a bathrobe on the air, because it was a Slumber Sunday segment. I also knew he was not wearing any underwear, because somebody had spilled coffee on his lap in the makeup room.

All of this knowledge was instantly contained within that single line, and it was just too much for fourteen words to hold, so I had to keep typing, or my mind would explode.

In my life, I had swallowed countless drinks and lit enough cigarettes to burn down the world; I had fallen in love and, once inside of it, spun around with my arms out-stretched and shattered everything; I had lost many things; I made mistakes; I made a single pot roast, and still my wrist held on to the scar. But one thing I had not done was this, whatever this was.

I was an advertising copywriter, though advertising wasn't writing so much as puzzle solving. I wrote in a diary as a kid, but my childhood felt impossibly distant. When I came home from rehab, I wrote, but that felt as messy as life. I had never seen a true and breathing world blocking my view of the computer screen. I had never experienced the draining of all I saw through my hands as I smashed down on the keys.

I did not stop writing until I could not operate my fingers any longer. Then I drank.

But I didn't reach the room, the place, the mind-set, the zone. Drinking failed me.

The next morning, which arrived much sooner than other mornings had, I sat back down at my computer in an uncomfortable chair, and I wrote again for as long as I could.

I drank that evening, but less.

The day after that, I wrote much later into the night and drank only what was in the neck of a fresh bottle of scotch.

On the fourth day, I wrote straight through all the sunlit hours, past the night, and into the pale early morning.

I forgot to drink. I just forgot to do it.

The sixth day of writing set off an electrical friction in my mind, and I remembered, *I can drink. I don't have to go out. Almost two full bottles.* This propelled me forward with a sense of joy. There would be no need to shower or dress or leave the apartment. I was spared my solitary humiliation at the liquor store cash register.

But I did not drink. There just wasn't room for it.

Because what was this? What the fuck was I writing? Who were these people, more of them on every page? How did I know about teleprompters and revolving television sets? Where had the knowledge of a Toys "R" Us store come from? Had I ever even been inside of one? These people who were exiting my fingertips; they were far more real than any I knew in the flesh. The things that happened while I sat in the bluish glow of my computer screen made me feel something harsh and addictive: alive.

Day seven was another twelve straight hours of writing, and then I stopped. Because it was finished. Whatever it was, it was done, gone. The spirit had moved through me.

I could drink now.

Except I didn't.

Because everything had changed.

I'd written a book. Whether it was a good book or a bad book didn't matter. It had chapters and page numbers and was, therefore, a book.

I could write a book. I had done it. There was proof of it just before me.

It was huge. I wanted to write another book immediately.

I didn't want to drink.

This was better. This carried me much further away from myself than drinking had ever managed to do. This should be a criminal activity, punishable by imprisonment or worse. The feeling it gave me was larger than the feeling of drunk.

I was in my underwear, and my bloated stomach felt

heavy and soggy as it rested on my thighs. I could smell urine. I could smell everything.

I was new. This was different. This was it.

I died.

I was born.

"You need a literary agent," Molly said. She had one herself and had just sold her first novel. Molly was an advertising copywriter, like me. We sent pieces of things back and forth to each other via e-mail. Parts of journal writing, pieces of ads. I sent her the messy writing I did when I was freed from rehab; she sent me sections of her novel.

"How do I get one?" I asked.

She told me to try her agent but try all the others, too. There was a book, a kind of bible of literary agents, though it more closely resembled a phone book and provided me with nearly a thousand pages of agent names and addresses.

It was shockingly overwhelming.

But now that I'd written what appeared to be an actual novel, I was devoted to finding an agent. Obsessed, really.

So I crafted a breezy and irreverent query letter and began sending it out in junk-mail quantity.

> *Dear Agent Person,*
>
> *My name is Augusten Burroughs, and I've just completed my first novel,* Sellevision. *Based on a QVC-inspired home shopping network,* Sellevision *is a satirical look at what might happen to the lives and careers of Sellevision hosts were*

*they somehow to be placed in the hands of a chemically im-
balanced writer with no apparent moral foundation.*

*Sellevision is a careening, left-field, neo-Shakespearean
romp that features a range of characters who experience everything from stalking to romance. It includes backstabbing, extra-
marital affairs, revenge, a porno career, and, of course, Debby
Boone, Joyce DeWitt, and Princess Diana key fobs.*

*It opens with the firing of an on-air host, the day after his
penis accidentally "peeks" out of his robe in front of millions of
viewers during a live Slumber Sunday segment. It ends with
the network in a delightfully ludicrous state of chaos. Either
that, or it's simply 45,000 words that don't belong together.*

*Obviously, I would love to send you the manuscript or
any portion of it.*

Thank you for your consideration.

Sincerely,

Augusten Burroughs

Most of the rejection letters I received in response were
polite—if not encouraging—but one asshole woman took
the time to scrawl a note at the bottom of her preprinted
rejection slip: "Satire is what closes Saturday night."

I only received rejection letters, and lots of them. With
one mortifying exception.

One agent did write back to me with something resem-
bling interest. He explained that while he, personally, found
the manuscript amusing, his colleagues at the literary agency
did not. He thought my novel needed a great deal of work,
but alas, he was not an editor. Finally, he said he'd be willing

to send it out "as is" to one or two editors he thought might possibly like it enough to buy it.

He then told me his literary agency charged for stamps and photocopies.

I was thrilled but also confused. It sounded like he was willing to lift a finger, but not two. He also had a long, old-fashioned-sounding name, which made me think he must be ancient.

I wrote to Molly and explained the situation. "Does he sound like a real agent? Why the fuck is he talking about postage stamps? Why do I have the sneaking suspicion he's just some old alcoholic living in a studio apartment in Hell's Kitchen, sitting at a computer in his underwear looking at kiddie porn?"

Only after I hit Send did I realize I had sent the message as a reply to the agent and not as a new e-mail to Molly.

Even though I immediately wrote a note explaining my grave error and saying, "Obviously, I don't deserve you or any other agent," I never heard back.

Two months passed with only rejection letters. One day, I got a form letter reject from a name I didn't recognize, as if I were being turned down by agents I hadn't even queried. I grew increasingly terrified that the agent with the old-man name I had called a pedophile might have been my single publishing opportunity, the big break I had been waiting for, and I had urinated on it by accident.

I considered the fact that drinking might lubricate my misery. I air-tasted a cocktail to see if one would just exactly hit the spot, and it was shocking to realize that I saw it would not. I did not want to drink. I mentally rummaged through my internal minibar: Jack Daniel's, Bombay gin, Absolut vodka, beer, chardonnay, crème de menthe; I didn't want any of it. And instead of finding this comforting, I found myself feeling abandoned. I had never before considered the possibility that I might never even want a drink yet still be left with this horrible, throbbing vacancy in the center of my being, right where my mental health and contentment were supposed to be.

On the floor of my closet was a box George's mother had shoved into my hands when she demanded the key to his apartment the day after he died. The box contained things she assumed were mine but which, in fact, were not. In it was a book, though, that George and I had bought together at the Barnes & Noble on Astor Place. We bought it because George's brother had worked for the publisher. I pulled it out of the box, which I now saw also contained the contents of the junk drawer from his kitchen, and carried it over to the bed.

It made me laugh. *Kept Boy* by Robert Rodi.

Something about it reminded me of my own novel. It was a satire, over the top, a little bit caustic around the edges but bighearted. It was a much more carefully crafted book than my own, that much I could see. But wasn't there some kind of kinship between them? Wouldn't a person who liked *Kept Boy* also like my own little *Sellevision*?

I e-mailed the author—this time without invoking Kathy Bates—and told him how much I loved his book. Then I admitted that I'd written my first novel, and because in spirit it was somehow similar to his own, I asked if he would mind telling me the name of his agent. Robert wrote me back right away and thanked me for praising his book. He also gave me his literary agent's name and e-mail address.

Unlike the other agents, this one replied to my query instantly, an amusing response that included the line, "Feel free to send me your manuscript at your earliest convenience."

I wrote back that my "earliest convenience" involved a wig, a revolver, and a stolen FedEx truck and I messengered the manuscript to his office on Eighth Avenue in Chelsea.

Several days later, he called and asked to meet for lunch at a restaurant near his office.

I was prepared for him to say, "What you've written isn't a novel. It's a cry for help." I remembered that was something Mitch's editor had told him about his last manuscript.

I did not expect this: him walking west toward me on Gansevoort Street, backlit by the sun as though he'd just stepped out of it, his thick, shoulder-length blond hair whipping around his face, sleeves rolled up to the elbows, a manila envelope tucked under one arm. His smile was almost too much.

"You must be Augusten!" he shouted from twenty feet. "I'm Christopher!"

In my mind, I chanted, "You will either be my agent or my boyfriend. You will either be my agent or my boyfriend."

I called out, "I hope I'm not late! It's great to meet you!"

He wore black-and-white checkered pants and a white shirt with no buttons and blue stitching. We sat at a narrow banquette in Florent, a cool downtown bistro, and we both ordered cheeseburgers, which came on English muffins. I eyed the envelope he'd slid beside him and wondered, did it contain a contract? Was he going to be my agent?

Lunch was going so well. He dipped his fries in mustard, and when some of it dripped onto his white shirt, all he did was laugh. "Oh my God, I'm such a pig."

He laughed almost constantly, nearly to the point of choking several times, banging his own fist against his chest. The tall, slender waiter refilled his glass with ice water, which he chugged as though it had been days since he'd had anything to drink.

He told me he loved my manuscript and that it needed "a shitload of work" but reassured me, "It'll be great, and you can do it. Totally."

I kept waiting for him to grab the envelope and hand me contracts to sign, because I'd read that's what agents did with new authors. But this didn't happen, and I began to wonder, so did all this mean he was my agent now? Or was I supposed to revise the manuscript, and then he would decide whether or not I was good enough?

I pushed my plate back and reached for my Diet Coke, which I sipped through a straw. I glanced at him, and he was already looking at me, smiling like he loved me. This made me look away from him and into the glass, where I stared at the ice. If he decided not to be my agent, I decided not to be a writer. I wanted this one, with the body of a wrestler and mustard stains on his shirt.

I found it both incredibly easy and incredibly difficult to sit next to him. I was funny around him; he brought that out. But I felt weirdly intimidated, too. If he wasn't going to be my agent, I wasn't fully confident I could even snag him as a boyfriend, either. Now that we'd had lunch, I was thinking he was out of my league, even with mustard stains.

He seemed so at home in the world, so comfortable and easygoing. He told me he'd been raised in Dayton, Ohio, but he seemed more like a California surfer dude to me. Plus, I'd never really been attracted to blond guys before, since I was blond myself. But he was a different kind of blond guy, a more durable variety, with the coarse arm hair of a Middle Eastern terrorist, which was exactly my type.

When he wasn't chewing and didn't have his mouth wide open in hysterical fits of laughter, I could see that he was actually extremely handsome. He did look like a corn-fed Ohio guy, now that I thought about him. He had symmetrical features, like a blond Tom Cruise. Once I saw this, I couldn't un-see it, and I also realized there was no way he'd date me. So by the end of lunch, when he still hadn't handed over whatever was inside that envelope and as we shook hands in parting, I felt a crush of despair.

I'd lost both an agent and a boyfriend at the same lunch.

Exactly like with an actual date, I kept going over it in my mind until I could no longer make any sense of even the simplest gesture. I was completely confused. Was it a good meeting or a bad one? Had he agreed to take me on as a writer or was I supposed to make those revisions first? And what were those revisions again? I hadn't taken notes.

When I got back to my apartment on Third Avenue and Tenth Street, I decided to send him an e-mail, thanking him for lunch and then adding, "By the way, are you my agent now?" at the very end.

Instead of writing me back, he called me two minutes after I hit Send. The first thing he said after laughing was, "Of course I'm your agent. I'm sorry. I thought I made that clear."

I told him I'd seen the envelope and kept expecting him to open it and hand me contracts to sign, a literary agency agreement.

He howled as if I'd just told the most side-splittingly funny joke. "Oh my God, I'm sorry. That was just something to read in case I had to wait. I can't believe you thought—" Then he set off on another bender of laughter. "This is an old 'handshake' kind of agency, but I will messenger you a contract. Yeah, you're my client, and I'm your agent, and we're gonna sell your book. Totally."

Totally. I hadn't used that word since the eighties.

As promised, he messengered the contract, and I spent at least twenty minutes holding it up to the light to admire the printed text, the texture of the fine linen paper, the logo at the top under which was printed "Literary Rights Management."

How was this even possible? If I had an agent, that meant I had to be an actual, real writer.

Along with the contract, he had enclosed a note. "I'll mark up your *Sellevision* manuscript with the changes and get that over to you within the next couple of weeks. Once it's good to go, we'll send it out. I know exactly the editor who's going to love it."

Two weeks and four days later, my manuscript arrived just as he'd said it would. I opened the box, and there it was, covered with red pencil marks. I paged through it and saw there were red slashes through entire paragraphs, complicated markings indicating I should move this line over there and take that line up there and put it at the bottom. There were tons of scrawled notes—questions, identifying plot holes, as well as technical stuff that real writers already knew (like "Each time a new person speaks, make it a new paragraph" or "There's this thing called 'dialogue' and you put it inside quotation marks"). He pointed out my strange yet consistent capitalization of words like Cake, Penis, Hostage, Meat, Police, and Gay—all things that made me excited and anxious, which seemed embarrassingly clear with each one he circled.

Every page was etched with his energetic scribble that at first seemed impossible to decipher, but once I sat down and studied, it actually made perfect sense and was like following a recipe. I realized the best way to make these changes was to question nothing. But in addition to moving things around and fixing my horrible grammatical errors, I soon realized I needed to write a great deal of additional material. As it turned out, I hadn't actually written a novel but something more like the outline of a novel. Now I needed to fill it in.

"Show, don't tell," he wrote. "Create scenes. Don't just talk about what happened."

I slept perhaps four hours a night for the next several weeks while I did nothing but revise my manuscript, because I was a writer now with a stocky, handsome literary agent who wore pants from the new wave era and said "totally."

I'd become addicted to his laughter. Each time we spoke on the phone because I needed clarification about one of his comments, something just clicked inside my head, and I found myself "on," and nothing else in the world mattered except making him laugh. At first, I only called once every few days, but soon, I was calling once a day and then several times a day, and he never made me feel like I was pestering him. In fact, it was just the opposite. He seemed thrilled to hear from me each time. And if he saw through my pale excuses—"On page 127, what's that word you wrote down at the bottom?"—he never let on.

All of me, each cell and membrane, every part of me was focused on one thing: making him laugh.

When I finally finished making the revisions and sent the manuscript back to him, it only took him overnight to read it. "It's great. It's fucking hilarious and sick, and Jen's gonna totally love it."

Jen was an editor at St. Martin's Press. He was going to send the manuscript out to a dozen editors, but she was the one he told me would love the book. He managed to get it into her hands right before she left for Germany for the Frankfurt Book Fair, one of the publishing industry's major events.

After two torturous days, he started getting responses. No, no, no.

"Don't worry. I still haven't heard back from Jen, and I know her really well. She'll get it."

My friend Molly tried to be supportive, but there had been a bidding war for her novel, so I wasn't sure she grasped my despair. "He says he knows just the right publisher," I moaned to her, "and now I'm pretty sure it's Kinko's."

At the end of the third day, Christopher called me. "I just talked to Jen from Frankfurt. She started reading it on her nightmare plane ride, and then when she got to her hotel and they had no room for her, she finished it in their lobby and laughed her ass off. She said everything since she left town has been a disaster except this book. Plus she's a TV home shopping fanatic, so she says nobody else can publish it except her."

I felt blood rush into my head and pound against my ear-drums.

"She won't be able to make a firm offer until she's back in the office, so she told me to give her until next week."

I panicked. "What if her return flight is shot down over the Atlantic? What if her jet lag wears off and she realizes her grave error?"

Christopher's way of reassuring me was to howl with laughter in my ear. "You are totally insane. She loves it. She's gonna do it. Just hang on until Monday, end of day."

Four entire days is a painfully vast expanse of time if you experience each second passing like one thousand one, one thousand two, one thousand three.

When I called Christopher at nine thirty Monday morn-ing, he told me to hang on, because he'd just walked in the door and had to set his coffee down and stash his briefcase.

When I called him at noon, he said, "It's not end of day yet, so, no. No word."

I asked, "Is no word bad? Should we have heard by now?"

He laughed again and told me, "No word means it's only lunchtime and she's rallying the troops, and she'll call with a firm offer by the end of the day, just like she said."

Three o'clock seemed "end of the day" to me, so I called him back. "I knew it was you," he answered.

Finally, at a little after five, by which point I had planned my memorial service, he told me the news. Jennifer had made an offer. "Seven thousand dollars," he said, his always-laughing voice suddenly betraying nothing.

"That's . . . not very much, is it?" I said.

"Not in the real world, no. But it's your first book, and they're really enthusiastic and just weird enough that they'll do a great job with it."

"Plus, I can buy a new wardrobe from the Gap with my advance."

Christopher said, "And with my commission, I can get a new pair of socks."

"So, did you say yes?"

He said, "No. You have to tell me if you want to do it."

I thought, *She could be changing her mind right now.* "Yes, yes, tell her yes. Hurry. Don't keep wasting time talking to me. Oh my God, you'll ruin my career before it even starts."

He said, " 'kay, I'll let her know and—"

"Hurry!" I yelled.

Four and a half minutes later, he called me back. "Okay, it's done. And I even got her to bring it up to a princely seventy-five hundred because I'm such a hard-ass. Congratulations. You just sold your first novel to St. Martin's Press."

I wanted to hug him, but he was on Eighteenth Street, and I was down on Tenth, so I stroked my thumb across the printed manuscript he'd marked up in red, making sure I only traced along his red pen marks.

"Thank you so much, Christopher. I just don't even—"

"Oh, my pleasure. Believe me." He barked out a laugh. "This has been a blast. Totally."

"So, what's the deal with you, boyfriend-wise? You seeing anybody?" I asked this as casually as I possibly could manage, given that the question was entirely out of nowhere. I was at Christopher's office because I'd lied and told him I had a freelance advertising client in the neighborhood. He knew I was earning money freelancing, so why would he suspect anything?

Slowly he said, "Am I *seeing* anybody?" Worse, when he said this, he stopped stapling; he just sort of froze with his hand poised over the black Swingline on his desk. "Where did that come from?" he asked.

I was wearing a tight T-shirt and jeans. I'd been to the gym that morning, so my arms were large. "Oh, I don't know. I just wondered. It doesn't matter." As a rule, if I am offered a choice between two things, I will take both and then run.

The truth was, it mattered enormously. Because over the past few months that he had been my agent and I had been his client, I had not been able to stop thinking about my alternate life, the one where he didn't agree to be my agent and was instead my boyfriend. I had begun to feel tricked, like I'd been paid $7,500 not to date him, and now it was seeming like I should either get way more money or get him.

He finished his stapling and then grabbed his coat from the back of the door. "Well, since you ask, I just broke up with somebody, a complete and total asshole, and I am so happy to be free of him."

I said, "Ouch. Sorry to hear about that," though mentally, I was high-fiving myself.

We walked back to Florent and ordered burgers again. This had become our routine; we met here at least once a week. Unless I stopped by his office for no reason, entirely unannounced, like I had done today. In which case, I might be able to sneak another lunch into the week. I'm highly sensitive, so I would have sensed—I believed—if I were being incredibly annoying. Which is exactly how annoying people justify being so insufferable.

It's possible my own internal bad-behavior radar had malfunctioned, but he never gave me any overt sign that he wished I would just go away, so I just kept at it.

It was here over burgers that he opened up about his life a little more, starting with, "I've been HIV positive since 1984."

In the time it took me to lower my glass to the table, an AIDS montage had played through my mind at methamphetamine speed: IV tubes, pumps and wires, tiny glass bottles filled with clear liquid, hypodermic syringes, amber bottles of capsules and tablets, pill splitters, pill boxes embossed with the days of the week, internists, specialists, bruised flesh, diarrhea.

"But I'm good. I stopped working for a while, just as the wave of new meds came along, so I never got sick. So far, they've kept me alive enough to eat cheeseburgers." He laughed and took a massive bite, the meat threatening to shoot right out the other end of the bun.

I said, "It's amazing that you're still healthy after being positive for so long." But what I was thinking was, *You just drove a stake right through the heart of my boyfriend fantasy.* After George, I would never again date somebody with that horrible disease. Or any other horrible disease, for that matter.

Instead of admiring the way his blue eyes flashed as he nudged his plate back with his elbows and exclaimed, "That was really good! Was yours okay?" I noticed he'd dripped something on the front of his shirt again. I pointed to it.

"Is that water?"

He glanced down. "Of course not. It's burger grease."

From this moment forward, I would take a careful inventory of all of Christopher's flaws, shortcomings, and abnormalities and create my own virtual catalogue of *deal breakers.*

The next time I was in his office, I watched him pull a step stool up to his bookcase to reach a title from the top shelf, and it stunned me. Was he short? What grown man couldn't reach the top shelf without assistance? That's when it occurred to me: he *was* short, actually.

"Oh my God, you're a short little troll," I called out.

He laughed as he said, "You're just noticing now?"

Obviously, I could never date somebody short. So even if he hadn't had AIDS, this short thing would have spoiled everything, anyway. I felt slightly better.

It had been nine months since I'd had a drink. This seemed impossible, and yet it was true. I hadn't attended a single AA meeting or counted days on my own. I hadn't read any books on the subject or had a spiritual awakening. I just hadn't reached out for a glass and then poured alcohol in it and gulped it down. I had not done that one thing. I had written a book and found an agent, and now my book would be published in mere weeks. It was at the printer, being churned out by the thousand, like Charleston Chew bars. It made the top of my head blow off to think about it, which is exactly what Emily Dickinson said can happen when you think about heavy shit.

I still felt blindsided by Christopher. In many ways, actually. He had become, by far, my favorite person in the world. Not just because he had plucked me from obscurity and was about to deliver me to the remainder bins of bookstores nationwide, though no doubt I was in his debt. It's that everything about him pleased me. I was funny with him. I could tell him anything. I could be my true, most horrible self, and he never withdrew. In fact, we grew closer, it seemed, by the day. His mannerisms fascinated me, and I was obsessed with his personal life away from the office because I knew so little about it.

Thinking about dating him and then learning he was medically off-limits still had me reeling, so I continued to find things wrong with him that I could point out. One day, he was wearing another of his complicated shirts with hidden buttons and fancy stitching, and I said, "What's with all the nursing blouses? Are you breastfeeding in the office?" Inch by inch, I became mean to him, but because he always laughed, my own meanness was disguised to myself as hilarity. Each snide remark or sarcastic observation was a handy little poker stick to ensure a certain distance between us was maintained.

I also realized, if I couldn't date him, I had to date *somebody*.

I saw that I'd never been my actual true self on a date before. Because my first book was about to be published and since writing felt like the thing I was *meant* to do, I felt almost virginal. It was suddenly breathlessly simple to ignore all my other failed relationships and terrible dates, because those happened to the old, unpublished, non-self-actualized version of me. They didn't count anymore. So I decided to troll some personal ads online.

I'd never had any problem with the concept of online dating, because how the fuck else can you meet somebody new without having to take a shower, leave the house, or brush your hair? It baffled me that so many people were still freaked out by the idea. Going on a white-water rafting trip was better? Out there in nature, the very place most manhunts for escaped serial killers begin?

I went to one of the popular dating sites that didn't just simply omit the option for male seeking male in their pulldown menu and then entered my zip code. My feeling was, if you're in the same zip code, you and I have enough in common.

Right at the top of the freshly sorted list was an incredibly verbose ad by a dude with salt-and-pepper hair and a great smile. Reading through his ad, I was charmed by how well written it was. It was funny, too, though I couldn't quite be sure if it was intentionally funny or if he was simply neurotic and befuddled by modern technology. But he could write, he looked great, and he was nearby. So I wrote him back.

He responded immediately but briefly. I wrote him a fat, long letter and pretended I was writing to Christopher so that I would be most myself.

He replied that he'd been planning on removing his personal ad that day and had just logged on to his account to do it because he'd received so many replies from the Philippines. This had infuriated him—"I said, 'NYC area only.' Can't people read?" He also admitted that my response had intimidated him and that he was only writing me back because he'd shared it with his business partner, and she'd told him, "You write that man back this instant."

This gave me pause. What had I said that had intimidated him and made him not want to reply? Then I thought, *It's good that I intimidate people. That's a compliment.*

His name was Dennis. After several back-and-forth e-mail exchanges, he suggested we speak on the phone. I almost never spoke on the phone anymore to anyone but Christopher. If he'd suggested we meet in person, I would have been game. But I realized speaking on the phone first had its advantages. Sometimes, somebody's voice just vibrates all wrong against your eardrums. Plus the whole "not taking a shower or getting dressed" part.

When we finally spoke the following week, we stayed on the phone for three hours. Technically, this is known as "hitting it off." To me, the next logical step would be to set up a coffee date. But Dennis felt we should continue with the phone for a while. He appeared to have an "if it ain't broke, don't fix it" mentality, and I reminded myself that normal, sane people are in no hurry, so I didn't push for an in-person meeting.

For the next two weeks, we spoke almost daily. Such concentrated, focused time on the phone with a stranger does peculiar things to the mind. You begin to conjure the person's physical being so intensely, you can nearly forget you don't know each other. You begin to tell yourself that no matter what they look like, the virtual chemistry you share is so powerful, it will be love on contact the instant you sit down across from each other at a rickety café table. But I was wise to this sort of brain trickery, because I'd dated, it seemed, most of the single guys in Manhattan at one point or another. Granted, many of them were indistinguishable blobs in my alcoholic smear of a social life, but I knew how the mind lulled you into a state of perilous complacency when all you had was a personality and a disassociated voice.

Meeting soon in person was essential. The longer we avoided this, the more likely it was I would loathe him. Looking forward to something with too much intensity was a total setup. I was reminded of being eight years old and seeing a "ghost" advertised in the back of a magazine for ten dollars. It took weeks and weeks for my ghost to arrive, and I felt each minute of those weeks. When at last it came, I was horrified to see that the ghost was nothing more than nylon string and a white plastic bag with two holes cut out for eyes. I had genuinely expected something vaporous and magical and ended up with a marketer's middle finger.

I was able to persuade Dennis to meet me at a Starbucks downtown after work. When he showed up, I was pleased and surprised that he looked as handsome as he did in his picture. Though, upon closer scrutiny, his mouth was on the small side, the corners downturned, and this lent him a minor air of generalized disapproval. This could be easily overlooked, however, because the way he trimmed his goatee optically enlarged the mouth, like a woman does with lip liner or an eyebrow pencil. This had to be intentional, and I had long believed that knowledge of one's deformities, flaws, or personal shortcomings frequently rendered them entirely beside the point. The sculpting of his facial hair to disguise his small, displeased mouth had to be rewarded by my own overlooking of it. And though he was not tall, he wasn't dwarf short, like inappropriate, medically and fashion-challenged Christopher.

We exchanged more e-mails after that first meeting. We had another date, and it, too, was a success.

Dennis asked, "Do you enjoy jazz? Because I love it, and I know of a place downtown where we could go."

"And then we can have broken glass and arsenic for dinner!" I felt like replying, because I barely tolerated jazz when I encountered it in elevators or dental offices. But I considered that when you meet somebody who *really* loves something, the high-road thing to do is to try to love it, too, so I wrote back, "That sounds great!"

We made a date for the following Friday.

In the meantime, I called Christopher. "Do you like jazz?"

"Not at all," he said immediately. "I mean, I respect it. It's a form of genius. But no."

"Would you date somebody who loved jazz?"

He took in a sharp breath. "God, no, of course not."

Christopher loved music intensely and had even recorded albums with a band. He played piano and told me he owned a black trumpet and a red accordion. His holiday mix CDs were legendary.

"What do you listen to?" I asked.

He said, "Oh, tons of different stuff. A lot of times, I just put my iPod on shuffle. Today on the subway, I listened to the Go-Go's, Slim Whitman, the Association, Steve Reich, lots of stuff."

I'd heard of the Go-Go's.

Dennis stood at the intersection of Seventh Avenue and Bank Street telling me he had a choice: we could either stay out all night and he'd be a mess in the morning or he could go home. He couldn't be drunk after just a few drinks, but he seemed tipsy and was in fact tipping over in my direction. Cars and yellow cabs rushed around us, a boxy blue-and-white Con Ed truck parked beside a manhole, lights were flashing, people were walking . . . the city whirled around and around us like a euphoric child.

The club had been larger than I'd expected and the jazz not nearly as bad, mostly because it could be ignored as we sat across from each other at a small round table with a votive candle in the center. The votive was the red glass kind usually found in standard-issue Italian restaurants, with little indentations like a child had pressed her fingertips into the glass all around.

Dennis seemed too shy to kiss me on the sidewalk, so I leaned in and kissed him. It was gentle, almost like he'd never kissed anyone before. His cheeks were flushed. Because of the wine or because he was nervous?

"I'll call you tomorrow," he said.

"I had a wonderful night," I told him.

He took the subway uptown; I walked home. I smiled

the whole way, which made me feel like a simpleton. I was a literal grinning idiot. No second-guessing, no wondering, *Is he secretly married? Was he only being polite?* Because these were the things we'd talked about, there was no need to worry about them now. How many times had I been on a date only to arrive back home and second-guess everything? Will he really call? I knew Dennis really would. Also, I'd already blurted out, "Do you have a terrible disease?" and he'd said no.

I was falling in love in Manhattan. We talked about falling in love in the city, how it just pushes you right over the edge. Falling in love in New York is dangerous for tourists, because they return to their split-level homes and they sit in their recliners and they look at each other and one or both of them thinks, *It must have been the Chrysler building.* But falling in love in New York is safe when you're here, and it never goes away.

One night, we sat on a long green bench in Central Park and talked until it was dark and the air throbbed with crickets.

He said, "Sometimes the feeling that I might be falling in love with you kind of slips away. Do you know what I mean? Does that happen to you, too?"

When I looked at him, healthy and strong, the only thing I could think was, *Please be the one.*

I said, "I don't know. Maybe a little. I guess feeling so much and thinking a lot about another person so intensely, it's like you wear that circuit down smooth in your brain, so all of a sudden, it seems like there's no feeling there. Maybe it's like a temporary kind of numbness. Is that what you mean?"

"That sounds like it exactly," he said. And he was smiling again, which relieved me. So had I said the right thing to diffuse his doubt?

When I was with him and he wasn't talking about the feeling slipping away, when he was smiling and telling me this felt too good to be true, I had a luminous feeling, almost like opening one of those tiny doors on the Advent calendar. You got to open one door a night until Christmas. It was small, but you knew it was leading somewhere.

I was on my cell phone with my appalling freelance advertising client when I walked past a Borders and saw a stack of yellow *Sellevision* covers on the front table. The phone just drifted away from my ear as the yammering continued, and I walked into the store.

"A novel by Augusten Burroughs."

It said so, right there below the title.

It was thrilling for maybe forty-seven seconds, and then the thrill drained right away. As I walked out of the store with my phone now in my pocket, I thought, *It doesn't matter what it is. We get used to it.*

Which is both good and bad.

It was almost two months, and I couldn't be sure, but I thought things were going well. Possibly they were even wonderful.

I was in love.

I swung by Christopher's office, and he was on the phone with a client. He motioned for me to sit, so I did. He was wearing a plaid, chocolate-brown shirt, and his hair was different. Blonder. Like he'd been in the sun.

While he talked on the phone, punctuating periods of intense listening with bursts of laughter, I fiddled with the loose paper clips, unforming them and using one to clean under my nail. I liked that I could be disgusting with him and it just didn't matter.

"So, how're things?" he said when he hung up.

I dropped the paper clip onto the floor so he wouldn't see. "Things are good. So. I'm pretty much in love with Dennis, that guy I told you about."

"Really?" he said. "Wow, that's fantastic."

He was smiling and looked really happy for me. Seeing this dented my mood. I didn't realize it until that moment, but I'd wanted him to be slightly jealous. But it just wasn't there.

"You seeing anybody new?"

He told me he was, actually. "And he's moving in."

"Moving in? How long have you been seeing him? And didn't you just break up?"

He laughed. "It's true. I'm a serial monogamist. Three weeks."

I just stared at him. "Three weeks?"

He smiled. "Yeah, I know. I move fast. Like a lesbian."

"So who is he?" I asked. I couldn't believe how not happy this was making me.

"His name's Zeke. He's crazy. And super tall. He doesn't

work, so there's that." He switched topics, but not as deftly as he thought. "But Dennis seems like a good guy from what you've told me."

I shrugged. "Yeah, he's a great guy, definitely. Okay, well. I should go."

When I left his office and started walking down Eighth Avenue, I thought, *Well, he really is off the table now. He's got somebody moving in.* Which was a weird thing to think, because hadn't I already taken him off the table? I was never going to be with somebody who was a pot of simmering AIDS stew again. No fucking way. So it was good. I was glad he'd found somebody and so incredibly fast.

He had somebody, and now I had somebody, too. It had worked out perfectly.

The only thing was, Dennis and I may have waited too long to have sex.

He was perfectly clear about his desire to not jump right into bed. He wanted to wait and allow feelings of affection and love to develop first. He'd told me this one night when we were out walking among the brownstones of the West Village. He said, "I've had enough sex with people just for the sake of sex. I really want sex to come from a connection with somebody I love. I want that intimacy."

This sounded perfect to me at the time. Given the trouble I'd had with Mitch, this was nothing but a relief. I felt confident that I would have no sexual issues with Dennis. Plus, because he wanted to wait, there was absolutely no pressure at all.

It seemed ideal until the day we actually had sex.

This occurred at a hotel because I had not yet cleaned my apartment to New Boyfriend Standards. So I rented a room at the UN Plaza Hotel. Two months had passed, and it was time to become, in Dennis's word, "intimate." And what could be sexier than doing it in a hotel with a World Health Organization rally going on outside?

Dennis's apartment wasn't suitable for sex, either. It was filled with boxes and two cats that circled my legs and tried to lick my eyes. They seemed feral to me, darting wildly around the apartment, pouncing, withdrawing. I'd asked their names, and Dennis said, "I haven't named them. I got them from this friend, Mary Ellen. She's one of those women who lives with like a hundred cats, and she couldn't keep these two extra ones, so I told her I'd take them."

I asked, "Do you like cats?"

Dennis replied, "Not really. Or, yes, I guess. They're okay."

"You should call them Licky and Clingy," I suggested.

He seemed depressed by the cats. "I've got to find a home for them. I just haven't had time."

It seemed he hadn't had time for a lot of things, including window treatments. What appeared to be burlap was tacked up makeshift fashion to his long wall of windows. It was a building from the 1960s, and nothing in his unit had been altered. It was a time capsule. The stacks of boxes added to this effect.

But my own apartment was worse, still a disaster wrapped in the remnants of my drinking ways. Piles of magazines and books needed to be thrown out or given away. The air itself seemed sullied. It needed a profound cleaning, and I needed to throw away a lot of crap, but I'd been sober for less than a year, which clearly was not nearly enough time to clean.

So, the hotel.

I checked in first and then called Dennis with the room number. He arrived about forty-five minutes later, looking out of breath and nervous. Because this was it. This was The Sex.

We undressed quickly, our backs to each other. Dennis finished first and climbed into bed, sliding under the sheet and then folding down the other side for me. It struck me as an oddly dated and feminine gesture, something from a Debbie Reynolds movie in the 1950s.

As I climbed into bed, Dennis said, "You have the cutest little flat butt. Almost nothing there at all."

He was smiling, like he was being playful and sexy, except to my paranoid mind, the smile lasted for one-hundredth of a second longer than a genuine "That's adorable!" smile would have, so it looked more like "No, I'm not disappointed *at all!*"

I said, "Oh, I know. I have kind of an anti-ass, don't I?"

"No, no, no, no, no," he protested, waving his arms. "I *do* think it's cute."

I said, "Okay," and I shrugged. "Then, thanks." I was feeling exceedingly awkward.

He admitted that he was a little nervous and asked, "Can we just hug awhile?"

I lay down next to him and felt relief coupled with a nagging postponement of some inevitable task. There was no getting around the incredible and puzzling awkwardness that

I felt. I mentally replayed some of our conversations and more romantic moments in order to remind myself that I knew Dennis; he wasn't just some stranger.

I slid down a little so that I could be shorter than him and then lay my cheek on his chest where the coarse, wiry hairs tickled my nose, and I kept fidgeting.

Eventually, we fell asleep like that, and I had the strangest and most vivid dream where Dennis peeled off his own face, which turned out to be a mask. And then he took this face off, which revealed another mask. And he kept going, like those Russian nesting dolls. All the while, I was fascinated by how many faces he had.

When we woke up an hour later, I was burning up, and so was he. I kicked the covers down, and we were naked.

We started kissing.

My dick was already hard because, as insurance against experiencing another erotic void like with Mitch, I'd clandestinely ordered a bulk supply of Viagra from an online pharmacy. I had been taking one before each date in case the evening spontaneously turned into sex. Dennis had no idea that when we went to that club in the West Village and sat at a small, round table near the stage, the entire time I was pretending to love crappy jazz, I was sitting there with a raging hard-on, weirdly divorced from any sort of sexual attraction. Also, the room was tinted Windex blue, and all the lights had halos. This was an actual side effect of the medication, one I rather liked. It turned the whole world faintly blue.

As Dennis's hand began the tentative journey down toward my dick, I smiled into his neck because I knew that he would not encounter the same cold, shrunken mushroom that Mitch had found on our second date.

The back of Dennis's hand brushed up against the underside of my pharmaceutically erect penis, and he said, "Wow, you're so turned on."

I was hard, that's for sure.

And I was happy in exactly the same way I'd been happy in 1983 when my friend Melissa and I were driving around at midnight on a back road in Hadley, Massachusetts, in my fastback, talking about how hideous our lives were when we just suddenly ran out of gas. Melissa completely freaked out because she'd already been raped twice, and she wasn't even twenty. She was trembling and turning around to check and make sure her door was locked, reaching across my chest to make sure mine was.

Calmly, I looked over at her, and I said, "I have a five-gallon tank of gas in the wayback."

Ka-boom. Total silence. And then a tiny and adorable, "Really?"

I was grinning, because it was one of the first times I think I'd ever felt proud of what was normally a psychiatric disorder: anticipatory stress.

I was always expecting the very worst; the bright side was that I was also prepared for it. Of course, I had a big red plastic jug of gas sloshing around back there. I had figured it would come in handy for lighting something on fire as I made a quick escape, but I was just as happy to use it for the good old-fashioned reason. I poured it into the tank and smashed my foot on the gas to flood the engine a little, and we took off, Melissa rolling the windows down and trailing her fingers through the wind like it was water rushing past.

Dennis negotiated new positions for us with me standing at the side of the bed while he lay on his back, his head hanging back over the edge of the mattress and my dick torqued downward into his mouth and throat. At the same time, I was leaning forward, propping myself up on my right elbow so that I could suck him.

My penis remained chemically, magically rigid.

A terrible thought crept in: *He's not very good at this.* And then I thought, *Or is he excellent and I'm just poor at receiving?*

I knew for a fact that I was excellent at giving head. This was perhaps the sole advantage of being molested at twelve by a skilled sexual predator, especially one who'd been through Catholic school and was, thus, a perfectionist. Over the years, I'd honed my skills and received many compliments, from judges to cabdrivers. Had I still been able to suck my own dick like I could when I was fourteen, it's possible I could have avoided yards and yards of shitty relationships.

Five minutes is a really long time to suck a dick.

After a while, you actually begin to wonder if the nonstop pressure against your lip-wrapped front teeth might, in fact, be loosening them. *If I end up having to have a root canal because of this*, I thought, *I will be really pissed.* Dental insurance doesn't cover blow job damage, I was almost positive.

At last, I sensed that he was about to ejaculate, and this, then, sped things up for me. We came at exactly the same moment. Dennis coughed after he finished, something I associated with guys who then said things like "I'd better get going. I have to pick up my wife's mother and sister at the airport in an hour."

We collapsed onto the bed, giddy with relief. The mystery of "What will the sex be like when we finally have it?" was over. The answer was: like assembling a bookcase from Ikea with parts missing.

"I've never come with somebody at the same time before, I don't think," Dennis said.

"It has to be a good sign, right?" I asked.

When there was no reply, I answered the question myself. "Yeah, I think it must be a really good sign."

I asked Christopher, "So what are you doing for Thanksgiving?" and he told me he was having a bunch of people over.

Christopher had lived in a massive rent-stabilized apartment on West Seventy-Ninth Street since 1985, and now Zeke lived there, too. Not long after we met, Christopher invited me to a birthday party for his ancient Samoyed, Ripley. I met a bunch of his friends, and it was like something out of a movie, all these funny, interesting people whom he'd known for decades. We all saw the deep insanity of throwing a party for a dog, yet it was still quite a sophisticated gathering.

I was the opposite. I'd lived in a series of junky studios for as long as I'd lived in Manhattan, and I was terrible at making friends. This was a lack that truly bothered Dennis. He'd even said, "I wish you were more social and had more friends you could bring to the relationship. I feel like I'm the one with all the friends."

And on Thanksgiving, I would meet several of them, because Dennis was hosting the holiday meal at his L-shaped studio on West Seventy-Second. The apartment had been improved since me: the boxes had been unpacked (and had contained mostly expired pens and stationery from an ancient job), and after several trips to Pottery Barn, it was slightly less pitiful.

I was excited. Normal, stable people celebrated holidays.

We went shopping at Fairway, and Dennis had already laid out several cookbooks on the kitchen counter.

I'd assumed cooking would mean throwing a turkey into the oven and opening a few cans of cranberry sauce while we lay in bed and watched pay-per-view until the guests arrived. But this was not the plan. The plan was for Dennis to create several painfully elaborate and complex dishes from *Cooks Illustrated*, using each skillet, pot, utensil, and pan at least once. My job was to remain fixed in place at the shallow stainless steel sink in his narrow galley kitchen with a scouring pad to wash and dry in a never-ending, one-man assembly line.

By the time the guests arrived, my hands were red, swollen, and steaming, but I felt I'd participated in preparing the meal; it was *our* Thanksgiving even though the table was populated with an increasingly strange group of strangers.

Sam and Paula seemed a normal enough couple, if a little grim. There was Stevie, a gay guy with tacky blond highlights, plus two single women who looked so remarkably similar I couldn't tell them apart even when I was seated directly across from them. The odd thing about Dennis's friends was that they all behaved as if they'd been dragged to this affair. Nobody spoke unless Dennis started the conversation.

"So, Paula, how's work?"

"Good. Busy."

Silence.

"Hey, Beth, I heard you went to Buffalo for vacation. How was it?"

"Nice. But cold."

Was I perfectly insane? Because I could not recall ever being among a group of such seemingly dead living people before. They were entirely joyless. Except for Stevie, who spoke in a kind of unwittingly comical gay slang. "So I told her, 'Girl, you ain't right!'"

Sam and Paula weren't married but had been together long enough that people assumed they were. They also bickered in hushed tones so frequently it was natural to assume they were not only married but headed for divorce.

"No, Sam, I said the pepper, not the salt."

"You said salt, Paula. Maybe you were thinking pepper, but you said salt. Anyway, they're both in front of you now, so take whichever one you want."

Dennis did a heroic job of keeping the conversation as light and as jovial as possible. Though it had seemed to be an inordinate amount of preparation—each measurement involved him sliding a knife over the top of a half teaspoon or quarter cup so it was perfectly, exactly level, not a crumb more or less—the meal really was delicious. The turkey even ranked up there with Mitch's Famous Author Friend's, though one did have to watch out for those small brittle sticks of rosemary.

"The food is spectacular, Dennis," I said, and this pleased him.

"I think the stuffing is a little dry," he said. "I should have used more liquid from the mushrooms."

There arrived a period of silence when people were concentrating on chewing, and it was during this moment that Dennis suddenly let out a high-pitched scream and covered his mouth. "Oh my God, oh my God!" he cried through his cupped fingers.

I tensed. Was he choking on a wishbone? Did he bite down on his tongue? Then a terrible thought: *Was there part of a rat in the creamed spinach?*

He shoved back from the table, shrieking, "My cap! My cap came off! Oh my God!"

There, through the gaps between his fingers, I could see a drilled-down stump right in the front of his mouth. I glanced down at his plate, and there lay one of the perfect, white teeth I'd so admired, stuck into a braised baby carrot, flecked with fresh mint.

Others noticed it, too, and there was stifled but audible laughter.

When he pulled his hands away, he forgot to close his mouth, so he looked like a hillbilly. I saw tears spring up in his eyes as he grabbed the carrot with its embedded tooth and rushed back into the bathroom.

He slammed the door closed, something he never did, not even when he had a bowel movement, I'd discovered. Dennis was a bathroom-door-wide-open kind of guy, which frankly freaked me out. That's how I knew just how upset he was; for him to actually close the bathroom door, this must be serious.

I felt terrible for him and considered rushing back after him, but something told me he wouldn't appreciate it. With Dennis now gone, nobody said a word, and I didn't even attempt to make conversation even though, as the new boyfriend of the host, part of my cohost job description was making conversation.

When Dennis returned several minutes later, he was smiling like nothing happened, his tooth restored to its central position. He took his seat.

"Sorry for the drama and excitement," he said, grinning. "It was this new crown. I was able to cram it back into place, but I definitely have to see a dentist."

Paula, whose cold bitterness rendered her less interesting than under-bed dust, remarked, "I had a silver filling fall into a bowl of Cream of Wheat once."

I thought but did not say, *Of course you did.*

Gay Stevie chimed in, "Sometimes, no teeth can be an advantage! I was once with an old man who had dentures, and let me tell you, when he pulled them out of his mouth, ooh, sister, that gent had certain, shall we say, *gifts.*"

The two women who I could not tell apart hadn't actually spoken. They'd merely offered meek smiles of either feigned interest or compassion, depending on the circumstances.

I was entirely miserable.

Was this really how it was supposed to be? Dennis had known these people for years. They were all normal people, and because they were his friends, they would soon be my friends, too. "Our friends." Normal people hadn't been molested or reared by a clinically psychotic mother, an alcoholic father, or a perversely mad psychiatrist who wore a Santa hat and performed toilet bowl readings. These were normal people, and I lived among them now. I thought, *This must be what I want.*

Over the next few weeks, I introduced Dennis to my very small collection of friends. There was Pete, an ex-boyfriend, and a former advertising coworker named Grace. Dennis and I had coffee with Sue, who owned a gift card company. We had dinner with Christopher and two writer friends. There was a great deal of laughter. Somebody snapped a breadstick, and the other half went sailing over to a nearby table, which all of us found way too hilarious.

"Your friends are great," Dennis told me. "See, you're not so broken."

Maybe I wasn't. When he smiled at me like that, I felt unbroken, and I felt safe. These were two things I thought I'd never feel with anyone. I cherished the feeling and longed for a lifetime of feeling so complete.

"I didn't know you had capped teeth," I said out of the blue. Ever since Thanksgiving, I'd been thinking about how the most surprising thing had been that he'd never mentioned them. But why would he, really?

He nodded. "Yeah."

I'd already unloaded my own inventory of bodily repairs, including multiple fillings, though no caps, and several re-stitched areas. He showed me his scars and opened up like a horse so I could see his rear fillings, but he hadn't mentioned the caps. Which was fine, which was nothing.

"Which reminds me," Dennis said. "You should make an appointment with the dentist. You should get a whitening."

"I should?" I said, mumbling.

"Yeah, it'd brighten your smile. You have a great smile," he told me. "Like when we were out with your friends at the Italian place. I wish you smiled more, in fact."

I made a mental note: smile more.

I made a second mental note: stop fucking obsessing about shit that doesn't matter. Because all of your other relationships? They failed. But they didn't just fail, they *fucking* failed. Stop screwing up your single chance at normal happiness by feeling testy when he tells you to smile more, which you absolutely should do. Stop thinking of dinner parties as threats. Stop being so damn *you*.

Dennis told me that his new therapist resembled "a soft cookie" with a pear-shaped body. At first, this was a description that I loved because it made the shrink seem completely nonthreatening, doughy but helpful. But it soon became apparent that the shrink was more cookie monster than cookie faced.

Dennis had been in therapy for over a decade, an achievement of which he was exceedingly proud. When he spoke of his years in therapy, it was as if he was speaking of having served with distinction in the armed forces. I wanted to point out that therapy was not a test of endurance, where the person who survived the most hours would win the mental health medal, but I wisely restrained myself.

His previous shrink had dropped unceremoniously dead of a heart attack. This new cookie-faced therapist had never met me, but I saw him as the enemy, because Dennis frequently returned from sessions with therapist-infused "concerns" or relationship script notes. He believed, for example, that our unsatisfying and increasingly rare sex was probably in direct response to the sexual abuse I had experienced as a child. I understood this was a logical conclusion, but I also didn't believe our sexual issues had anything to do with what happened to me all those years ago. I'd worked through that shit, was my feeling.

The therapist was also worried about my lack of closeness with family and my history of alcohol abuse. *If only he could meet me*, I thought, *and I could explain myself.* I engaged in discussions with Dennis during which I said things like "It's smart for your shrink to be wary of you becoming involved with an alcoholic. But remember: I went through treatment at a drug and alcohol clinic in the Midwest. And even though I relapsed, I've been sober for nearly two years." When what I wanted to say was, "Tell the Pillsbury Doughboy he can take his rolling pin and use it to shove his advice up his ass."

It was an eggshell thing. If I expressed too much resentment, I knew it would get back to the shrink, who would say, "Didn't I warn you? He's maneuvering to drive a wedge between us and sabotage therapy." So I had to play along and be as encouraging as I could about Dennis's therapy while at the same time try to subtly glean as much information about the sessions as possible, without resorting to a microrecorder dropped into his briefcase.

"Why," I wanted to ask him, in the kindest way possible, "after so much therapy are you so wishy-washy and insecure?"

I thought back to the table. *God. The table.*

After Thanksgiving, that very evening as I was transferring all the dirty dishes into the small, narrow kitchen for a marathon, nightlong session of washing, I noticed that each time my fingers so much as glanced the surface of the table, it jiggled. It was just a cheap throwaway table, the kind a college kid might have. I said, "We should get an antique table, one of those big, really solid things. Wouldn't that be great?"

Dennis had been deeply wounded. He remained silent the rest of the night while I was doing the dishes. And I'd assumed he'd fallen asleep, but in fact, he was awake and going through my comment over and over in his mind. He'd finally screwed up the courage to confront me.

"I feel like you think my choices aren't good enough for you, and I'm resentful."

I tried to explain, "This has nothing to do with your choices; it's just about the table. It's not solid, you know? Didn't you feel it at dinner, sliding around under our plates? Remember when Blanda actually apologized to it when she bumped it and made it jiggle and the waters sloshed out? Apologized . . . to a table. Plus, don't you love old things? That's all I meant."

Dennis smirked a tiny bit. "Her name is Brenda, not Blanda. And I remember," he said, biting on his lip so that he didn't actually smile.

I loved that I could make Dennis go from grumpy to almost happy. It made me feel like the only thing he'd been missing his entire life was me. It made me feel like I was good for him. He'd been single for so long, and the more I knew him, the more I saw the loneliness at his core. I felt like I brought him to life.

He made me feel stable and safe.

This reminded me of what magazines and therapists were always saying about relationships: people should complement each other.

Like us.

We did end up buying a large, old table, and Dennis was extremely happy with it. "You were right about this. Now I'm embarrassed that I ever had the other one."

But that exchange stuck with me, because after more than ten years of therapy, a person really shouldn't be so inextricably emotionally invested in his or her table choices.

I would need to work harder to loosen him up even more.

My new relationship with Dennis was different from my previous ones, or at least it felt different, because I was sober and actually experiencing it. Dennis was normal and stable, and he enjoyed things I felt I ought to enjoy, too, like National Public Radio and classical music. In fact, I was feeling so positive that I decided to write him a letter, which I would present to him on our one-year anniversary. The point of the letter was to playfully demonstrate that I had been right all along.

I begin by writing, "When you date a writer, you should get love letters. This should be one of the fringe benefits."

But that evening, I felt a little drained after writing almost fifteen single-spaced pages of things like "And the weird thing is, when you glared at that woman for cutting in line in front of you with her smiling and blushing, 'Oh, pretty please? I just have the one package of dates?' I could totally read your mind, and I knew you wanted her to be assassinated, because so did I!"

So I drank one of my revolting cultured enzyme drinks that are supposed to make you smugly healthy, and then I went to sleep.

The Jeep Guy was waiting for me. This time, he was turned a little sideways in the seat of our same Jeep, and he had a playful expression. He was gripping the wheel right as he shifted into first.

"Better hold on to something," he said, my only warning. And we were back on the trail almost on our backs it was so steep. This time, there was music I'd never heard before, and I loved it and wanted to know who it was. His answer made no sense to me. It sounded like Radio Waves Are Not a Color. But in this dream, he was gunning the engine, and we were climbing faster. I still felt like he had done all this before, and I was on his home turf, not mine. I still felt at ease, and was it in love? Maybe I was a little edgier this time around. I was asking questions.

"Are you sure this is a safe trail?"

But my only reply was laughter—not mean but rather intimately, affectionately tolerant.

When I woke up my first thought was, *Something must be wrong with me neurologically.* Such a specific dream, so vivid and impervious to the wasting effects of time, it couldn't just be a normal dream. Now it was an officially recurring dream, for one thing. Though I still did not know him from my waking life, I was absolutely certain that Jeep Guy was real, that he didn't just exist in my dream world. He had gotten to know more about me. He was expecting my slight paranoia. And he was totally fine with it, charmed even, maybe. When I woke up this time, it was even harder to settle back into wakeful reality, because I had experienced what felt like love. Something so powerful it could be nothing else but love.

Because I had committed to sharing myself fully with Dennis and containing no secrets, I told him about the dream, plus the first one I'd had a couple of years before. I explained how vivid they were.

Dennis was into dreams. Hearing other people's dreams didn't bore him; it fascinated him. And he seemed really good at reading the deeper meaning within them.

"I think it's obvious," he said as he scraped toast crumbs off the table and into his palm. "You are this Jeep person; he is you. He's the rugged, capable, and confident version of yourself. You're merging with him. You have been for years. That's why it's been a recurring dream. I think it means you're becoming your truest self. It's about growth."

This sounded exactly like the sort of thing you'd be able to say after spending so many years in therapy. It sounded perfectly possible, actually. It was an interpretation far too reasonable for me to ever have thought of it.

But pressing against my skull in this matter was the insistence of what I felt: *No way. Jeep Guy isn't me. He's Jeep Guy.* Perhaps I needed the fairy tale to remain in place that my dream contained a message or a destiny and was not, as Dennis said, evidence of my own growth. It seemed silly now to think of Jeep Guy as anything besides my own best self, as he had been all along.

For several weeks, we had sex once a week. But swiftly, the sex tapered off so that we only had it once a month. This seemed slightly troubling, considering this was still supposed to be the whirlwind falling-in-love stage of the relationship, where everything was as good as it was ever going to get. True, he was busy with his business, and I was working on what would be my next book, and it was a little crazy jumping back and forth between his apartment uptown and mine in the East Village. So we were stressed out. But there were rumors people even had babies under such circumstances, so it seemed like a couple of guys could pull it together enough to roll around a bit.

Dennis mentioned one evening that he preferred black men to white men.

He said this casually as he peeled away the outer leaves of the brussels sprouts. We were in the kitchen, and I was helping him prepare dinner by cleaning things or handing him level teaspoons of whatever he needed.

"What was that?" I asked.

He said, especially if they're bodybuilders with huge asses.

I was not black and didn't look like a bodybuilder. A kind, honest friend once told me I had the body of a tube sock.

Dennis then admitted that for years he'd carried on a sexual relationship with a black man in Harlem. "Prior to knowing you," he added.

"How prior?" I asked.

"Pretty prior," he replied.

He reached for a copper-bottomed saucepan and asked me to hand him the olive oil. I also did this casually, wearing a small and artificial smile.

"There was nothing between us intellectually. In fact, I didn't know anything about his life. All we had was intensely invigorating sex."

I thought, *We're doomed.*

Looking at his closed, focused face as he dumped the brussels sprouts into the pan, I knew that asking him for details would only make him hostile, which he would then mask with additional silence and a tight smile.

I cupped my hand on top of the counter and scraped the discarded leaves over the edge into my other hand and tossed them into the trash.

"So, do you miss him?" I asked.

Dennis turned around and opened the refrigerator. He didn't say anything.

I felt an uncomfortable, hot pressure in my chest waiting for him to answer. "Hmmm?"

He said, "I miss some of the things we did together. Yes."

I rinsed my hands because it was something to do. "So, what does that mean? You thinking of seeing him again?"

The question seemed to offend him. "No, I'm not thinking of seeing him again. I don't even have his number. I threw it out when I met you."

In his hand was a jar of pickles.

"What are you doing with those?"

He noticed them. "I was moving them out of the way." He placed the pickles back in the refrigerator and closed the door. "I have no interest in seeing him again. That's not why

I brought this up. But I can see that I probably shouldn't have, because now you're accusing me of doing things."

In the old days, back before I was a sober, published author in a healthy and mature adult relationship, I would have lashed out with something like "Look, asshole, nobody is motherfucking accusing you of anything except being a complete and total dick." But my own ways hadn't worked, and my sorry alcoholic instincts just couldn't be trusted, so instead of lashing out, I pulled off the road.

"I'm sorry," I told him, moving close. "Honestly, I didn't mean to make you feel accused. That is the last thing I meant to do." I hugged him and felt his stiff, angry posture relax. "I know you're not seeing anybody else. I'm sorry."

I'd finally cleaned my apartment and bought a feather bed, along with new sheets and a comforter at ABC on Broadway. It was smaller than Dennis's place, but the bed was larger and way more comfortable. So lately, we'd been spending more time down there.

It was a little after midnight, and I hadn't heard from him since we'd spoken early that afternoon. I knew he had some kind of conference or something after work, but we were supposed to see each other after that. He told me he'd be finished by eight.

I finally just spoke the words out loud to myself. "Is he with the guy in Harlem?" Dennis had described him only as his "former fuck buddy" and claimed to know almost nothing about him even though they had a physical relationship for over a decade. Though one thing Dennis did tell me about him was that the guy had gone to an Ivy League college and worked in academia. Because I had so few actual details about the man himself, I had to invent them: six-and-a-half feet tall, sculpted from muscle, the color of bittersweet chocolate, and with a penis the diameter of a baseball bat. In my mind, he was also a classical musician and stand-up comic. He held a gray metal box with a red button protruding, and when he pushed the button, Dennis got a shock in the ass and dropped whatever he was doing and took a train up to Harlem to lie on his back and throw his legs up in the air.

I suspected he'd either slept with this allegedly retired fuck buddy again or was going to sleep with him that night. Then I wondered, is he actually in love with the guy? Several times, Dennis had spoken of his attraction to African American men. But was this attraction just a general preference? Or maybe did it center around one particular African American man?

I thought back to our awkward conversation on the phone that afternoon. It had been somewhat stilted, polite. Impersonal. Like he was somebody from customer service and we were chatting it up.

He was far more upset today than he let on, I thought, *and I think something is coming to a head tonight.* This would explain why I had been in such an outrageously foul mood all day long, unable to do anything except dwell. I thought, *I have known somehow. Picked something up. Understood on a level not quite conscious.*

It was after two in the morning when Dennis finally showed up at my apartment. He was sweaty and clammy and looked exhausted. He said he was late because he went out for drinks with a girl after the cocktail party in midtown, and then he went back to his office and sat in a chair in the dimmed lights.

"I did some thinking."

That sounded much worse than taking the subway uptown to see his former fuck buddy. No good ever comes of sitting alone in a dark office and thinking. Next to "needing some space," perhaps "doing some thinking" was the worst phrase to hear from somebody you were dating. The words filled the air with grim reaper–breath incense.

"Just alone? In the dark? What were you thinking about?" I had to ask even though I suddenly felt narcoleptic and like I wanted to crawl in the closet and sleep under the coats.

Dennis undressed, removing his shirt and draping it carefully over the back of my desk chair. He removed his pants, aligning the creases in the leg, folding them once, laying them gently on top of the arm of the couch. This undressing struck me as unspoken good news: Who gets undressed before storming out of a relationship?

He came over and sat on the bed. "I was thinking about us. Nothing new. Stuff we've talked about already. Sometimes, I just wonder if I'm not meant to be in a relationship. Like I just don't know what I'm doing. I worry about us being so different."

"I worry about that, too," I told him.

The relief on his face was instant. "You do? You never told me that."

"I do think about it, but I don't worry so much about it,

like you do. I guess I feel more like we complement each other."

Dennis put his arm around me. "We do complement each other, you're right. And I love you."

When he was warm and open like this, I loved him and wished I could put a freeze on the moment, make it longer, make it stay.

"I thought you'd say, 'Fuck it,' and that would be it—we'd be finished. I wasn't expecting you to say you also had doubts."

I saw that his eyes were moist.

I leaned into him, but what I thought was, *Wait*. Was that what he really wanted, for me to say it was over?

Why did I feel like he was holding something back?

I supposed I was holding back, too. In the last twelve hours alone, I went from feeling incredibly close to him to feeling like we would break up the next time we were together. In fact, I constantly expected it. But then I always expected the worst and tried to prepare for it.

My brain got broken a long time ago, and as a result, a car driving along the street is never just a car driving along the street; it's a death machine with eroded brake lines, and the driver is sneezing and doesn't see that he's careening toward me. So many years of anticipating disaster is exhausting. Though I have tried to train myself not to think this way, it never works, so plan B is to go ahead and think this way but then remind myself I'm wrong. Which means I can only cobble together a life by clobbering my faulty "gut instincts" 100 percent of the time.

Soon, though, the relief on Dennis's face melted away and was replaced by duress. "I was thinking something else tonight," he said.

I had the sensation of being on a roller coaster, the part where it suddenly dips.

We were seated in bed, propped up against the pillows.

"Do we move in together? Do I need to see you every night?" he asked.

I looked at him to try to read his face. He looked sort of miserable. As though this were a question of which of his children should be taken off life support.

I thought, *Is it really so terrible? The possibility of living together?*

"I'm just very new to this, relationships," he said. "You're more experienced than I am. I've never been in something this serious and intense. I just don't know what we do. I don't know if my feelings are okay or if they mean something."

I wanted to say, "Yes, that's what we do. We move in together." But I didn't say this, because Dennis was all about taking things slow, and it was *still too soon*.

And it would be *still too soon* for the foreseeable future. This was, after all, a man whose last official date had been ten years earlier. If he could go a decade between dates, he could certainly allow thirty or forty years to pass before deciding we should share a mailbox. So he threw the relationship ball back into my court because I was "more experienced" in terms of relationships. If failed relationships and blackout sex count as experience, that is.

Just when I thought he was finished confessing all the things he'd thought about when he was alone in his dark office, he admitted that he had a desire to go back to his old life.

"Not that I would, but I have to admit, I think about it sometimes. It's tempting."

He shot me a guilty blush when he said it, so I figured he was talking about getting fucked by the African American Adonis. Which meant I'd been half-right. Maybe he hadn't actually been with the guy, but he'd been sitting in the dark daydreaming about it.

Dennis stared down at his lap. "I hope I have the courage to continue with us," he said.

I smelled a setup. Now he could break up with me without conflict. He could, in the days or weeks to come, simply reveal that he lacked the "courage." In this way, continuing would be impossible, the fault entirely his. Maybe I was being paranoid and this was more of my piano-falling-from-the-sky kind of thinking, but it seemed to me Dennis had just laid the groundwork for an incredibly polite breakup.

I sank back against the pillows. I kind of wanted to scream and bash my head back against the wall and jump out of the bed and run somewhere.

I was so confused.

I was in love with him.

I wanted us to live together, because he made me feel safe and secure. Except? What I was feeling now was the opposite of safe and secure. So what did he make me feel?

Sleepy.

It's so hard to really trust what's inside another person, to really believe someone's intentions and what he or she says. I wished I could just trust him completely, without my own constant doubts regarding his constant doubts.

One clear autumn morning, I arrived nearly a half hour early for my nine o'clock chiropractic appointment in Soho. This happened because I gave myself forty-five minutes to travel from Dennis's apartment on the Upper West Side to Spring Street, a twenty-minute commute. Because of my unbridled anxiety about being late for anything, I am accustomed to being laughably early for everything, so I figured I'd walk around the neighborhood looking at the sparkly sidewalks, dented trash cans, and homeless meth addicts. But this turned out to be one of those days where each actual second seemed to take numerous additional seconds to actually pass. After ten minutes, I felt like I'd been walking for a week. I wandered into a Starbucks and ordered a double espresso. Once I had the hot little paper cup in my hand, I wondered why I'd even ordered it; I didn't really like espresso, though I did like swirling it around in the cup and watching the caramel-colored foam stick to the sides.

I gulped it down in one bitter and semiscalding swallow, tossed the cup in the trash on the way out the door, and was walking along Spring Street when a woman shouted from a window overhead, "A plane flew into the World Trade Tower!"

She was screaming this over and over. It seemed like I should be able to see her hanging out the window, but I couldn't. She was just a frantic voice. I assumed she was drunk. Who else would hang out the window before nine in the morning and scream things onto an empty street?

It was almost nine. The espresso left a bitter aftertaste.

I wandered to the corner of Prince and Mott to see if anything had actually hit one of the buildings. I walked slowly, one step above bored.

There was a low playground across the street, and this was why I could see straight downtown. The World Trade Tower was venting a column of black smoke as thick as the building itself.

As I stared, the top of the other tower exploded.

I love a good disaster. News coverage of a plane crash will keep me glued to the television without sleep and only very rushed bathroom breaks. But as I watched the towers burn, I felt something sharpen within me. This was the realization that I was not merely watching the spectacle of disaster occur on my wide-screen television; soon I would smell smoke. It instantly stopped being fascinating and amazing and became real: horrifying and impossible but happening, and what *was* happening?

And something else.

A nagging sensation.

Had I left the house without my keys? I slapped at my hips and felt the keys in my left pocket. What, then? The oven? Didn't use it. What was it?

Dennis. But what about him?

I was hypnotized by the smoking towers. The woman wasn't screaming out the window anymore, and the street was empty. Where were the cars? The towers burned and churned out roiling blackness, and the fact that I was watching this happen did not in any way make it seem like it actually was.

I remained rooted to the sidewalk, feeling the heat from the flames on my face, which was impossible. I wondered if more buildings in Manhattan had exploded. Was this the end of something?

Dennis?

He had left before me in the morning to go to his therapy appointment at eight thirty.

My brain prodded me. "And where was Dennis's therapy session?"

The answer crawled forward slowly, as if there was a delay in my ability to think. Dennis's therapy session was downtown. In the World Trade Center.

I turned away from the towers. Immediately, I felt clear and focused. My nose decongested. My back did not hurt.

Dennis would be walking out of therapy soon, and he would exit the base of the building not knowing that it was burning. Pieces of tower would be falling to the ground, burning. He could be hit with debris. I thought, *I have to go downtown and find him.* Then I thought, *I'll be able to find him. It will just happen.* I would be able to find him, because I have always been able to do things that seem unlikely or even impossible.

I jogged over to Broadway. The WALK light was flashing, but I stopped. It would be chaos down there. Of course, there would be no way to find him amid the destruction and commotion.

People on the street were sobbing and pointing. They were screaming. Some were running.

Dennis was to meet his business partner uptown at the apartment at ten. I would go there, and when she arrived, we would take her car. If she hesitated, I would buy her car from her on the spot, drive downtown, and find him that way.

I saw a cab. Impossibly, it was free, so I raised my hand, and it veered over to the curb and stopped hard. I gave him the address uptown, and as he drove, we were in salute; hundreds of people lined the streets, hands raised seeking cabs.

I tried my cell phone, and it did not work.

My body chemistry began to slow as I realized, with an awful finality, that Dennis could be dead.

The radio said the word *terrorists*.

Fire trucks and ambulances were screaming downtown. Of course it was terrorists. I hadn't even paused to consider the *why* of what was happening. If a dinosaur stomps onto your lawn, you run. You don't stay in the pool and go, "Now wait a minute, just how did you . . . ?"

The cab was making all the lights, but I still wasn't home. I called it *home*, but it was really Dennis's apartment. I was destined to return to my filthy studio alone. Because I loved him so much after having lived a life without love, after having only needed, that is why I would lose him. I needed him too much, so he'd be taken away now. I was happy. The rug, therefore, must be pulled.

The cab reached a clog of traffic near midtown. We stopped moving, and I wondered, *Is this what it looks like? The worst day of your life, moments or hours or possibly even several days before you realize in retrospect this was the moment when every-thing changed for the worst?*

My mind went in a circle, clockwise: me not hearing from Dennis today or tomorrow; Dennis not coming home because he is not alive.

Finally, we reached the apartment building, itself a sky-scraper, and I ran inside. The lobby was packed with senior citizens who had ambled down from their apartments to gather and wring their hands. I strode over to the elevator banks, hating their slowness more than ever and then feel-ing a sting of surprise and gratitude when there was an el-evator already waiting. I pressed the button for our floor and then caught myself holding my breath.

My hands were shaking when I unlocked the door.

It was empty.

He was not there.

And *wait*.

The TV was on. His briefcase there on the floor, tossed.

And Dennis *walking around the corner*, his precious face, all mine, his expression numb, so much damage in his eyes. No dust on his body, no blood, clean, pressed and whole.

I rushed into him, pressed my body against his, hard, not hard enough. He smelled like him.

Anything else can happen to me and I don't care, I real-ized.

What can you say? I said, "Thank God." And I do not believe in God. Except, for this fleeting, thirty-second window of my life, I did, because he brought Dennis home unscathed.

He was bewildered. "I had the wrong day," he muttered.

"I went downtown and realized I got my days mixed up. So I went into Century 21 and bought some socks. Then I got back on the subway and came home, and Alice called from her car and said, 'Turn on the news.'" He showed me his receipt from the downtown clothing store: he must have taken the last subway to ever leave the World Trade Center station before it was all crushed to rubble and dust.

Standing side by side, we watched the towers fall on CNN.

If his apartment had faced south instead of north, we could have watched without a television.

I led him into the narrow, windowless kitchen. I backed him against the trash can by the wall and held his face in my hands. I said, "I want to spend the rest of my life with you. I want us to be married."

Dennis closed his eyes. He said, "Okay."

I said, "Are you sure?"

He nodded. "You should get rid of your apartment downtown and move in," he said in a numb monotone. He turned, walked back over to the TV, and stood there watching.

I looked at the back of his head, salt-and-pepper hair buzzed close to his scalp, and thought, *That's it—we're official.*

I looked down at the worn linoleum floor. I decided to clean and wax it. I used a small brush I found under the sink to scrub it on my hands and knees. Briefly, I wondered, *Is a terrorist attack a poor reason for taking our relationship to the next level?* But he'd said yes, so I didn't want to question it. How rash could my suggestion have been if he'd agreed to it? Dennis was a bit of an emotional penny pincher, after all, kind of a cheapskate when it came to handing out the feelings.

Still, as I slopped liquid wax over his barely there, worn-out kitchen floor, I couldn't help but think it was like a macabre game show. Maybe I'd won, but would I even want the prize? *"It's the end of the world! Grab whoever's next to you and bury yourselves under the trash in the backyard! Hurry!"*

After the grisly stench—electrical fire mixed with meat and blended with chemicals—left the city and spring had finally arrived, the area was renamed *Ground Zero* and became something that seemed permanent, a macabre construction pit on a vast scale, nothing to be visited. Life simply continued without it.

One morning as he stood in the steam-drippy bathroom trimming his soul patch with a small pair of scissors, Dennis told me that he wished I made more of a social effort. "It just feels like I'm the one who's always making plans with other people or suggesting we go to the museum or whatever."

What he said was completely true. I was totally happy watching common TV with him, having no friends, and eating only food from takeout cartons. This, I suddenly saw, was a character flaw.

Instead of looking at me in the mirror when he said this, he leaned in close to inspect the precision of his trimming.

"Sometimes it feels like that," he added in an offhanded way, offering me a tight little smile. "Just once in a while, you could suggest a bike ride, or maybe there's a book reading you'd like to go to."

The only thing more distasteful than riding a bike would be riding a bike to a book reading.

I folded my arms across my chest and felt very drowsy, like I might actually nod off while standing there in the bathroom doorway.

I stared at the back of his head and wondered if there was something else. Sometimes, his criticisms came in sets of three, like sneezes.

"All right, so you wish I was more fun, basically. What else?"

He didn't answer. He just returned his prissy little scissors to the polished glass shelf of the medicine cabinet and closed the mirrored door. Then he splashed water on his face and patted it dry with one of the stupidly expensive hand towels that were perfectly folded beside the sink. When he finished, he said, "I think in every relationship there are things each person wished were different."

So what else bugged him besides the fact that I didn't throw enough fondue parties? I mentally rolled up my sleeves. I thought wearily, *Is it always going to be like this with him?* He was like a vending machine that swallowed my change and wouldn't give me my fucking peanut M&M's.

"Well, could you maybe name something? Or a few things? Because you seem a little distant, and if I don't know what I'm doing wrong, how am I supposed to stop doing it?" I trailed him out of the bathroom, practically tugging at his sleeve like a toddler.

In fact, he'd seemed slightly distant all week. Perhaps all month, actually. Possibly longer. I'd let go of my place downtown, and we were living together now, so this was it. It had to work now.

He closed his eyes and extended his tongue between his

lips before speaking, a gesture that struck me as annoyingly mannered. "Well, as a matter of fact, I can name something. It bothers me that you never seem to want to leave your, you know, *computer*."

He said the word *computer* as though it was an entirely foreign object, something newfangled and impossibly dangerous to everyone around it, like talkies or the automobile.

It was true, of course. I was perfectly content to let a beautiful, sunny weekend pass unappreciated outside the window while I lay in bed with my laptop on my stomach, e-mailing friends and eating cheese popcorn. I'd lived in New York City since 1989 and never visited the Empire State Building, the Statue of Liberty, or the Central Park Zoo.

I also had two herniated disks and a spinal stenosis. Eleven back specialists, each more learned and expensive than the last, told me there was nothing I could do except continue to take pain medication and wait for it to get worse. This situation made it hard for me to even bend over, let alone stand in a museum. Or ride a bike. I felt that this was a perfectly legitimate medical excuse and that I should be allowed to remain indoors forever.

Because I had not yet spoken, Dennis interpreted my silence as a possible acquiescence. He continued. "I also worry that you're reverting back to your old ways." His face flushed as he spoke.

"Old ways" was his code phrase for the period of ten months before I met him, when I was a bed-wetting drunk, alone in my apartment, sitting at my computer in my underwear.

In a way, he was once again correct. I was reverting.

Only instead of drinking, I was writing. I saw this as progress. Wasn't it? I wasn't in my underwear anymore; I wore gym shorts.

I was sober and in a relationship, and that was supposed to be better than being a drunk, but I also felt like, at least when I was a drunk alone in my apartment, I didn't feel like my walls resented me or wished I was something other than the mess I was.

Molly was also a writer, so I asked her, "Do you ever leave your house? Are you happy to always stay inside by yourself?"

She wrote back, "This was always a bone of contention in my marriage. Philip married a writer and then wondered why I wasn't out water-skiing."

This made me feel better for a moment, until I reminded myself that Molly and her husband had divorced. It turned out he had a secret girlfriend along with a new baby on the side. I wondered if he met her water-skiing.

I used to guilt-trip myself when I was a kid. *You have to stop lip-synching in front of the mirror. It's a beautiful day. This is not natural. Bring a hand mirror outside and use the sun as your spotlight if you must, but you need fresh air.*

The thing is, I wanted to be more like the person Dennis wished I was. Dennis had the soul of an accountant, and he was exceedingly good at cataloguing my flaws. And because I contained mostly flaws, it was daunting. I had good parts and pieces, too, but these aspects of my character attracted way less attention, possibly because they didn't require renovation.

I wanted to be somebody who made plans and had friends and knew when the farmers' market was in the neighborhood. I wanted to be spontaneous and informed. I wanted to somehow just know when the Chuck Close exhibit was at the Met and then have the motivation to go. As opposed to suggesting, yet again, that we have sandwiches and watch old movies on TV—and not even toasted sandwiches, because that's just extra work for nothing.

I wanted to be *that guy*. Or perhaps I merely *wished* that I wanted to be that guy. Wanting to want something isn't the same as wanting it. I suppose what I really wanted, then, was to give more of a shit, because about certain things, I simply did not.

Dennis would have been so fucking thrilled if I only suggested we do a triathlon together. He would have gone into training immediately. Not that there's anything wrong with people who do triathlons for pleasure. It's just that I have absolutely nothing in common with these people. In fact, I have a great deal more in common with serial killers. I am not a triathlon kind of guy, and I don't want to be one, either. Dennis's idea of being a couple meant doing things together. My idea of being a couple meant being together but not doing anything except laughing at the couples who were out there doing annoying shit together. If I could attend the finish line of a triathlon and photograph the assorted leg injuries and bodily swellings, I might enjoy it.

He had said he didn't want me to shut myself in. He was

terrified (his word) of us becoming "isolated." What alarmed me is that his idea of *isolated* was much closer to my concept of *ideal*. If we lived on a great expanse of land, Dennis would want a grand swimming pool so that we could invite all our friends over for long, leisurely weekends. Whereas I would want a moat filled with saltwater crocodiles to keep the riff-raff out.

Much to my surprise and slight alarm, Dennis and Christopher formed a friendship independent of me. On the one hand, this was good, because at least Dennis was spending time with a quality person, something he had few of on his own. It also made me seem more valuable in that I had someone worth stealing. I came to the relationship with a built-in agent! Who was fun! Besides, it gave the impression that I had sanctioned the friendship but had better things to do than go out for long, loud, laughter-filled dinners.

The first time they had dinner without me, I stomped around the apartment, alternately anxious and enraged. *Are they talking about me? They'd better be, and it had better be flattering. I hope Dennis doesn't say anything that will let Christopher know what I'm really like. Fuck, I hope they're not talking about me. They'd better not be.*

When Dennis had not returned by midnight, I knew for certain that they had figured out that I was extraneous, they were having an affair, and I was about to lose a boyfriend and an agent in one dinner I didn't even get to attend.

I fleetingly considered that Dennis had been mugged and was lying on some side street with broken ribs and no wallet, but the mental picture was too appealing at the moment. When I finally heard his keys in the door, I quickly flopped on the bed with my laptop, as if I'd been lounging there for hours, not caring that I didn't end up with the blond literary agent *even though I saw him first.*

I needn't have moved with such great haste, because the door unlocking took quite some time, what with all the key fumbling and dropping (twice) before he lurched into the apartment. If I'd lit a match at the other end of the room, I could have set fire to the liquor fumes emanating from him. He dropped his things on the dining room table and saw that I was still awake. "Oh, hi!" he yelled, like someone wearing headphones who can't modulate his or her volume. "I didn't know you'd still be up."

Hoping he'd take the hint, I spoke very quietly. "Did you have a good time?"

A hint was way too subtle for someone this drunk. "It was so much fun!" He started detailing the food they'd ordered, which was not the information I wanted, but I listened dutifully.

"So you were at the restaurant this entire time?" I asked, trying not to let judgment creep into my tone, as if Mr. Distillery Breath would notice.

"No, no, no. We finished dinner a long time ago and then went out for a nightcap."

Nightcap. It was another of those suburban 1950s concepts that seemed learned from TV or movies, not from the real world. It implied "just one more," which appeared tonight to have been "just one more bottle." It seemed unlikely that he'd seen Christopher naked or that they'd plotted my murder, so I just let him natter away while he got ready for bed.

If he was this smashed, I wondered what shape Christopher must be in. It's widely known that Little People can't hold their liquor, so he had probably passed out in a cab on the way home. I opened a new e-mail and sent him a quick message: "Hey, how was dinner?"

Mere moments later, I got his response. "It was great. Dennis is really sweet, and I see why you like him. He's stable and handsome and smart—and boy does he know his way around a bottle of wine. Or two." He then launched into a work issue that had come up while he was at dinner, saying he'd handle it in the morning. It all seemed disturbingly sober, especially since Dennis was already splayed out next to me snoring while Christopher was planning my career. Seemingly nothing could penetrate his shield—not AIDS, not liquor, not even a demanding, crazy author.

As Dennis thrashed and turned on his side before he began snoring again, I reminded myself just how deficient my agent would be as a boyfriend.

Dennis rented a car so that we could take a road trip out to Pennsylvania to visit his father who lived in an ingenious on-demand assisted living condominium unit. If you were relatively healthy and didn't need any medical assistance, it was just a small efficiency apartment like any other. But if you suddenly developed a health issue, there was a white-clad medical staff on hand 24-7. You could go from living an independent, carefree lifestyle of board games and craft projects one day to being ventilated and on life support the next without ever having to leave your own unit. Dennis's dad was popular, and as we were leaving the building to go out for lunch, two other residents engaged him in a brief conversation.

I whispered to Dennis, "I wish we could live here."

"I know," he said. "This is great. You know what's best about it?"

At the same time, he said, "Laundry service," I said, "IV morphine."

We decided to take an alternate route back to New York, because the highway between Pennsylvania and Manhattan was such an endless stretch of tedium. We used the car's GPS, but rather than guiding us, it kidnapped us. After four hours, we realized we'd been heading south, not east. At first, Dennis was furious, but I held his hand and told him it was a good thing.

"We'll check into a Bates Motel and eat Kentucky Fried Chicken in bed."

This pleased him enormously. Dennis loved eating messy food with his hands, but only when nobody else was around so that his face could be unapologetically covered with grease.

Later, we snuggled up together on the small, hard mattress with the bleach-scented sheets. We were somewhere in Virginia. My face was pressed against his neck.

"Don't move," I told him. "This is perfect."

"I won't," he said, hugging me closer. "It is."

"Do you think we should search the room for peepholes?"
I asked.

He smiled. The room reeked of chicken. I was happy.
Dennis was happy. I knew this, because I asked him, "Are
you happy?"

"Yes, I'm happy."

But I wondered. "Would you tell me if you weren't?"

"I would tell you if I wasn't happy," he said.

I couldn't leave it alone. Was it *happy* that I felt? As I lay
against him and aligned my breathing with his, I realized
the thing I actually felt was *safe*. Normal people who weren't
raised by mentally ill goats probably took the feeling of safety
for granted. They only noticed when they suddenly felt *un-
safe*. When the hands reach up from under the bed and grab
their ankles, they scream, whereas I'm like "Wait, can you
scratch my knee before you kill me?"

Expecting the mushroom cloud, I am stunned into blinking stupidity when I look at the sky and see only blue sky.

I realized I was thinking about all of this because feeling
safe felt almost like drinking; something I could imagine
myself becoming addicted to instantly. A feeling I would
need to experience constantly, no matter what, from now on.

When Dennis had his first colonoscopy, I went with him to
the appointment. When it was over, I joined him with the
doctor for the results.

"Everything looks good," he told us.

The doctor was about Dennis's age and actually resembled

him with short, salt-and-pepper hair and coordinating closely cropped facial hair.

"That's a relief," Dennis said.

The doctor then did something doctors don't usually do: he made small talk. It was doctorly small talk, but still. "Anything else on your mind? How are you feeling otherwise in your life?"

By the end of the appointment, we knew that the doctor enjoyed photography and also played guitar. He was like a friendly family doctor from a Country Crock margarine commercial, except his office was within gunshot distance of the E train.

After we left, Dennis raved about the man. "We should become friends with him. He was amazing."

It's true, I thought. *We should become friends with the man.* Because like a vampire, I wanted to suck the charisma from his veins.

Over the next several weeks, I increasingly felt that Dennis ought to be with a well-adjusted proctologist instead of with me. An easygoing professional who didn't hold a grudge against the sun and had his own scrapbook of recipes clipped from *The Times* over the years. I likewise worried that my true mate was somebody who was definitely out of prison but maybe on house arrest for the rest of his life because he did something absolutely awful but thrillingly interesting and unique. Or maybe somebody with a fatal sun allergy. I would love the psychological permission to draw the shades during the sunniest, most glorious day of the year so I could stay inside and type. And not feel like I was deeply defective for this. Or, at least, that I was deeply defective but, so what? Pass the chips and salsa.

I also understood that I had to expand myself as a person. Because this simply would not do, this innate character of mine.

Dennis had expanded himself by giving up his design business to become my business manager. We were an actual corporation now, with a joint checking account and letterhead. Instead of sausage casings or urinal mints, our company created books. Technically, I created the books and earned all the money while Dennis managed it and told me when I could buy a new laptop or upgrade my cell phone. It was like I finally had the dad I never had.

We were together forever. Dennis was my security.

So yes, I would expand as a person. And Dennis would simply have to understand that I could only expand so much before I burst all over the dinner guests and stained their lovely outfits with my mess.

Though I almost never visited the place, I did own a small house in Northampton, Massachusetts. While it had originally been built in the 1930s—the period in architecture responsible for the Empire State Building and Frank Lloyd Wright's Pennsylvania masterpiece, Fallingwater—my house had possessed but a single charm: a low asking price. It was not the quaint, graceful abode one might expect of a home near the banks of the historic Connecticut River.

I bought the house before I knew Dennis. Which is to

say, there was nobody to stop me from buying it at the time. My inspiration for purchasing it: inevitable doom. It would be my emergency bomb shelter, purchased with book advance money. If all failed, I figured, I could return to the town where I was raised and live in the most inexpensive house on the real estate market. It had been so affordable because the street was in a declared flood zone. At the time, this seemed like no big deal. I thought, *So I'll live on the second floor.*

Decades ago, it had been a farmhouse with modest charms. Then it was gutted and renovated by the previous owner, a man who clearly had no more experience with home renovation than I did. As far as the craftsmanship of his work was concerned, at least the new vinyl windows were not upside down. There was not much to say beyond that.

Any original details, such as pretty crown molding or solid wood doors, had been stripped clean out and replaced with their contemporary particleboard equivalents from Home Depot. I knew nothing about the man who owned the house before me except the color of his pubic hair and the fact that he must have had a tremendous amount of it, because I was vacuuming those curly red fibers out of the beige wall-to-wall carpeting for a year.

There was a large island in the kitchen with a white laminate top, new oak cabinets, and electrical outlets in abundance, making *handy electricity* one of the home's prime selling points. The sliding glass doors off the kitchen overlooked an expansive boggy field where one could easily hide among the shoulder-high weeds. I figured the place would be perfect for the future emergency me; the failed single writer who had become destitute and was now hunkering down until an asteroid hit the planet.

The fact that the house was devoid of charm meant it was easy to maintain. After all, where there are no window boxes, there can be no flowers to water. Aluminum siding meant the house could remain pristine white for all of eternity. But even a plastic wineglass of a house, as it turned out, was a tremendous amount of work for somebody who heaved heavy sighs of fatigue and annoyance when he had to lick an envelope flap and then carry the envelope all the way outside to a mailbox.

The narrow strip of dirt and weeds that separated my house from the street was in fact a Rorschach test for the rest of the nosy neighborhood, who apparently viewed it as an actual lawn—one I was expected to care about and maintain. Notes were slipped under the screen door. "Hi. I just wanted to let you know that my son could mow your lawn if you like, for ten dollars, every two weeks. I only say this because your yard is a little unruly."

Ignoring passive-aggressive notes like this was a specialty of mine, so I welcomed my neighbor's "thoughts." Even though I was rarely at the house, it made me feel secure to own it. I just never expected that I would one day need to expose a boyfriend to it.

When Dennis first saw the place, his distaste revealed itself on his face in the form of furrows and frown lines, even though his mouth evicted the words, "It's cute." Which was exactly what he said the first time he saw my flat butt and tried to mask his disappointment.

"It does have a luxurious number of outlets in the

kitchen." I smiled expansively, just like the Realtor had done with me. I even made the same sweeping hand gesture.

"I guess that's a good thing," he said, frowning.

But as much as he loathed my little house, he did like being in rural Massachusetts. And because my career hadn't failed as I'd expected and because I was now part of a couple instead of part of a suicide pact with other survivalists, we decided to sell my little house and build our own new, vastly superior house in the next town.

Construction took almost two years. The doors were solid. The trim was wood, not Sheetrock. The shingles were cedar instead of aluminum. From nature's point of view, our new house was entirely edible.

One unexpected benefit of suddenly owning a new house that required as much attention as a newborn was that we now traveled between the apartment in New York and the house every weekend. It wasn't that I enjoyed the three-hour drive, but now we just didn't have as much time to spend with Dennis's soul-numbing friends, and this secretly delighted me. For the most part, I saw them as placeholder friends, waxworks from a cobwebbed museum of people he'd accumulated over the years without much thought given to their actual personalities. If there was a trait they all shared, it was a peculiar emotional remove that made interactions with them puzzlingly impersonal. I felt certain that chinless Brenda, whom he'd known for over a decade, couldn't even spell Dennis's last name. And on the rare occasions when one of his friends called him, it was usually because they were dutifully returning his call to them.

"It's not that I hate your friends," I lied. "It's that none of them seem to have any real affection for you. It's almost like they're generic."

Dennis felt I was making him choose between me and his friends; I felt I was making him choose between actual friends and a bunch of names in an address book.

There were exceptions. His South American friend, Marta, was smart and filled with life; she adored Dennis. And his former business partner, Alice, was fun. But for every Marta or Alice, there were four or five Gray Garys. Gary's skin was actually the color of a fly's wings. I once had to sit across from him at dinner while he described the difficulty he'd experienced opening a jar.

His wife had joined the discussion. "I told him he should try running the lid under the hot-water faucet," she'd said in a voice just barely above a mumble. I could never remember her name, so I dubbed her Tedia.

Gray Gary said, "So I did like she said and ran the lid under the hot water. I had to dry it off because the water made it slippery, you know?"

Dennis nodded enthusiastically, like this was the most scandalous story he'd ever heard, positively dripping with suspense and intrigue.

"And then once it was dry, I was finally able to twist it off. Seemed like a lot of trouble to go through for some pickles," he said in thrilling conclusion.

Tedia added, "They were those pickles sliced lengthwise, for sandwiches."

Because I am a horrible person, my eyes bored through her skull as I sat there smiling and thinking, *Oh my fucking God, please stop talking about pickles. Please stop breathing. Nobody in the world cares about a single mushy word falling out of your face, so at least shut up so I don't have to look at your tan teeth.*

It was sometime after this endless dinner when I realized that almost all of Dennis's friends seemed clinically depressed. Lumpy Tina, whom I'd only met once and had forgotten by the time I turned away from her; Pat, who lived in suburban Pennsylvania and collected plastic food storage containers; Roxy and Chaz, whom I at first presumed to be a lesbian couple on the verge of breaking up were in fact man and wife, newly married.

The exception turned out to be Sam and Paula, whose low-level bickering at Thanksgiving barely hinted at the real fireworks. They had recycled their depression into a glorious and spewing volcano of unbridled rage. A salty cracker could provoke an explosion of "I need a fucking knife to scrape off all this goddamned salt. You could melt the snow on every road in Connecticut with these bastards. Christ."

Sam and Paula fascinated me, because all they did when we visited them at their eighties time capsule of an apartment was complain about the unfair downsizing they experienced and scream at each other over the tiniest and most insignificant things (cheese and dust were favorite topics) while their nine-year-old son lay on the carpet in front of their chipped glass coffee table and drew unicorns with his crayons.

I didn't want Dennis to get rid of all his friends. What I wanted was for him to have friends who were more emotionally engaged with him, called him for a change, asked him how his life was going, showed some actual friendship. If that meant all new friends, I couldn't help it.

"Why do they always look like unhappy rabbits?" I asked Dennis once after we left Sam and Paula's apartment.

"I didn't think they looked that unhappy," he said unhappily.

I turned to him. "Didn't you ever see *All About Eve*? That's Marilyn Monroe's line; she says it at the party. Are you sure you're even gay?" I added with a smirk.

There was a muscle twitching in his tightly clenched jaw and a slight narrowing of his eyes that let me know he did not find this funny. He coughed.

I could watch old movies all day every day for the remainder of my life. What was wrong with a black-and-white world? Dennis preferred decorating shows on home improvement channels, which hurt my eyes and my sensitive, broken brain.

Once we started living together at "our" apartment uptown on Seventy-Second Street, Dennis's 1950s-white-person-movie behavior became terribly apparent—his defining trait, even. He began leaving notes on my laptop keyboard on his way out to work or for a run, notes that said things like "Pick up some butter today!" or "Vacuum a little if you have time after you finish writing?" Sometimes he even drew a smiley face on the note. Other than a question mark at the end of a declarative statement, a smiley face is the most passive-aggressive form of punctuation known to man, and Dennis knew how to combine the two.

I was painfully aware that it was still entirely *his* apartment even though I now lived there, too. None of me had permeated the space. His tacky African baskets hung on the walls, his wobbly bookcase threatened to fall over onto the floor like a drunk. I just hadn't felt like I could pee on his hydrant, so I still felt like a visitor. It was different when we went to the house in Massachusetts. Because we'd created it together, it felt a little more mine.

The first week I moved into the apartment, I stood to answer the phone, but he intercepted. "I should probably get that," he said.

"Oh," I said and stepped out of the way. *He wants to be the one who answers the phone. Okay.* He also wanted to be the one who controlled the music: smooth jazz, twenty-four hours a day. I looked at it like, *That's okay. I can give up music. I have to write, anyway.*

When the phone rang one night just before midnight, I thought it was probably him since he'd been out at a friend's birthday dinner, but I wasn't sure it was him, because sometimes his father or his sister called. So I just stood there in frozen stupidity, looking at the damn phone as it trilled atop his Ikea buffet.

Finally, I picked up, and the first thing he said was, "What took you so long to answer the phone?"

I couldn't just blurt out, "I was worried it might be one of your tedious friends, and I'd get stuck talking to them for even thirty seconds," so I said, "I was cleaning the toilet." Which wasn't a lie, only a time shift, because I'd scrubbed it earlier. On my actual knees.

"Well, I wanted to let you know I'll be home soon," he said.

There was something odd in his voice that I couldn't positively decipher. Something that reminded me of our early dating days when he was worried about slipping out of love with me, as though love was a pair of jeans and he'd been on a juice fast for a year.

He told me he was getting ready to leave the party, but he was helping them clean up; all the other guests had already left.

I wanted to tell him, "The hosts never want help cleaning up; they just want all the guests to go the fuck home so they can polish off the wine and talk about everybody," but I didn't say this.

He told me, "I'm really tired." But it didn't sound like tired. Was he drunk and trying to hide it?

I said, "Okay, so you can go to sleep when you get home."

Why was he calling me to tell me he was tired? It made no sense.

And then, why my paranoia?

For the past couple of years, I had fallen into a permanent bad mood. An endless male PMS. Suspicious, anxious, second-guessing myself. It seemed I was so constantly wrong about him that I could no longer trust my own instincts.

When Dennis had looked angry several days before and I had asked him, "Are you angry?" he replied, "No, not at all."

Score: Dennis 1, My Instincts 0.

I pressed the issue, which was seemingly of my own creation. "Are you sure you're not angry?"

He chuckled. "Of course I'm sure. But I might *get* angry if you keep asking me."

So he definitely hadn't been angry, and I definitely had believed he was. This meant something inside of me— something I had relied on my entire life—was essentially faulty. My compass, my inner homing pigeon, my deepest instincts.

Since mine could clearly not be trusted, I would have to rely on his.

My third book had just been released, a memoir about drinking, called *Dry*. I'd actually written it before *Running with Scissors* or *Sellevision*. It began years earlier as a journal when I got out of rehab and didn't know what to do with my hands or my brain. If I went downstairs for five minutes to buy cigarettes at the Korean market and the guy handing me back my change accidentally touched my hand, that's what I wrote about for the next two hours. I lived a small, desperately sober life where I did pretty much everything wrong and microexamined every petty detail until I could at least understand myself better. It didn't become a book until I'd given it to Christopher and asked him, "Is this style of writing anything I could ever use somewhere?" I wanted to know because my journal writing was so different from my *Sellevision* novel writing.

His reply had been, "Why didn't you show me this first? It's amazing."

I said, "That's not even possible. It's just my own mess."

"Well, yeah," he agreed. "You need to cut about seven

hundred of these thousand pages. But it's a memoir. I think Jen will buy it."

I was astonished, because it seemed like he was going to ask my publisher to buy my used tissues, and that could ruin everything. Of course, once they found out that my childhood was even more fucked up than my adult drunkhood, it was decided that *Running with Scissors* should be my next book. It was after that that I released *Dry*, the first book I ever wrote, published as my third.

The alcoholics and drug addicts had come out in force to meet me and share their own sordid stories of debauchery. It was surreal and amazing and also totally draining and exhausting. After more than a month on the road, I was completely spent and just wanted to be hospitalized in traction because my back was killing me. I was also willing to accept being placed in a mental institution for several years, where I could learn to knit. But I'd promised Dennis that we'd take a vacation. "Just as soon as my tour is over," I'd told him.

Dennis didn't truly grasp the magnitude of my double life. On the one hand, there was the me that he knew: motionless on the bed with my laptop, my entire circle of friends seemingly existing only within the computer itself. To him, I seemed perfectly content to live as a shut-in.

Then there was the other me, the writer who met thousands of new people every year, who signed voluptuous breasts with black markers (by request—I wasn't just running around with a Sharpie looking for boobs), attended cocktail parties with booksellers, exchanged brief though intense moments of brutal intimacy with stranger after stranger for weeks at a time.

I tried to explain it to him. "You think I'm antisocial, but I'm incredibly social; it's just that it all happens in a very compressed period of time."

All he saw was the former alcoholic, spending yet another day in his gym shorts, tapping away on his keyboard, for all he knew looking up recipes for mixed drinks like the Harvey Wallbanger, the Singapore sling. That's how he looked at me, with a side eye that said, "You're up to something over there. I don't know what it is, but I'm watching you."

We'd added two smash-faced dogs to our little family, and the hardest part about being away from home was being away from them. But a few days after finally returning home and curling up into a slumbering pack, we handed them over to Christopher, who had plenty of dogsitting space in his rambling apartment, and flew to Amsterdam.

People were surprised we chose Amsterdam of all places. "But you're sober now. Why go there?"

Because I'd thought exactly the same thing myself, I could only reply, "That's where Dennis wants to go." The fact that he wanted so much to see Amsterdam made me want to go there, too.

He was looking forward to the museums. Which to me translated to: standing in line for hours only to then spend more hours standing around in front of walls. Museums were not my thing because it hurt my screwed-up back to stand. If I could rent a stretcher and view museums from a horizontal position, they would totally be my thing.

Though I was half-excited to visit the Anne Frank house. In third grade, only the girls got to read *The Diary of Anne Frank*. All I knew was that there was some lesbian material in the book and that the house had a hiding space behind a false door. I am all about false doors.

Arriving in Amsterdam was disorienting. Everybody rides bikes everywhere, which I supposed was admirable and inspiring, but it felt like stepping into a buzzing haze of flying monkeys. I was almost hit by some asshole healthy person every two and a half seconds.

Then there were the tangled, guttural vocalizations the Dutch people made to form their own private little language. Dutch isn't easy for the outsider to learn, because it's spoken from the back of the throat at the trigger spot for the gag reflex. In order to make the correct sounds, you have to have quite a bit of phlegm at the ready, which is probably why everybody smokes. Nonsmokers can't even understand Dutch, let alone speak a single word of it. The word for "hello!" is actually the noise you make when you clear your throat really hard before hurling out a loogie onto the ground. "Have a nice day" sounds exactly like someone choking on his or her own tongue.

The smug Dutch learn three languages in school, because they know that nobody else in the world is going to speak their strangled and gasping mother tongue. They learn the extra two languages, I figured, to show off. I was onto them: in my experience, startlingly modest, peaceful people would do anything to get you to notice how startlingly modest and peaceful they were. The Dutch did not fool me any more than the Buddhists I'd known growing up in western Massachusetts. Give a Buddhist a vacuum cleaner and the very first thing he or she will do is run through the house with it, sucking up all the spiders. Zen, my ass.

According to the itinerary Dennis had devised and then printed into an actual stapled handout, we would trudge from one continent-sized museum to another before embarking on a lengthy barge tour (with an onboard wine tasting for him) of the meandering canals and then finally to the Anne Frank house and its concealed hiding place. The itinerary was two single-spaced pages and resembled a publicity tour. Seeing it, I thought, *If I made it through thirty days of rehab, I can make it through two weeks of Amsterdam.* I was counting days again, just like in the early part of my recovery.

On our first night, we went to dinner at a sleek and modern restaurant housed on the ground floor of one of the narrow, stepped-roof houses that line the canals. The juxtaposition of the several-hundred-year-old canal house and its contemporary, glassy interior was almost pleasing enough to make up for the fact that the room was filled not with air but faintly blue cigarette smoke.

Dennis had something misleadingly called *steak*. When the plate with the scrawny piece of meat landed on the table, I said, "Looks more like pounded canal rat."

He ate it dutifully, insisting, "It's not that bad. It's actual steak; it just probably comes from geriatric cow."

Because the Netherlands is a coastal land, I ordered fish. This turned out to resemble a small, Chinese hand fan on the plate, just a splay of slender bones stretched with thin, translucent fish meat.

Dennis washed his blackened strip of deadness down with wine. I made a meal from the ice of my Diet Coke and ate all the bread from the basket in the center of the slightly wobbly table. As I watched him drink, his face visibly relaxed, which made me think, *Well, of course.* I hadn't expected to want so desperately to drink in Amsterdam, but this was precisely what I wanted to do. I even said to Dennis, "The really fucked-up thing about being an alcoholic who doesn't drink anymore is that on days when you really, really need a drink to take off the edge, all you get to do is wait for the edge to pass on its own."

He looked horrified, like I'd admitted to pushing a little girl into a canal when he'd turned his back. "Edge?" he asked. "What edge? We're on vacation. This is supposed to be fun. I'm sorry you're having such a miserable time."

Now I had to backpedal. "I'm not having a miserable time," I said, sucking on my straw at the loud dregs at the bottom of the empty glass. "It's just, well, you're having wine. That's all. I wish I could have some, too."

"You've never said that before," he told me importantly. "You never talk about missing your drinking days."

"Oh my God," I said. "I don't miss my drinking days." He had no fucking idea. Urine-soaked mattresses, spider hallucinations, sex with taxi drivers, and just endless chaos—I didn't miss that shit. "It's not that big a deal," I said. "Just forget it."

What I wanted to tell him is that I felt like a dog who had just been informed that all of the treats in the world have been recalled, but it came out as "Just forget it."

On the way back to the hotel, I stopped at a small neighborhood store and bought an emergency sack of pastries. It was startling how my mood improved by encountering an actual tower of assorted baked goods right there on the counter next to the cigarettes and roach clips. I had already begun reading my copy of *The Diary of Anne Frank*; now I would spend the evening learning about how she had to eat boiled potatoes and wilted cabbage soup while I lay in bed eating chocolate tarts and sugar waffles.

Things were starting to look up.

After leaving the store, we saw some action: two blond officers, one male and one female, dragged a belligerent drunk down the street. The drunk screamed at the female officer and then, in a move of shocking dexterity, managed to kick her by somehow bending his leg around hers. She let go and moved behind him, allowing her partner to maintain his grip, and then she ran ahead, positioned herself just right, and kicked the drunk motherfucker right back, causing him to scream and fall forward, clutching at his stomach.

Dennis crossed us to the other side of the narrow street, because it looked like the ranting drunk might actually break free from the blond cops and bite everybody nearby, but I wanted to jog up closer to watch the Dutch lady cop beat him up and then roll his broken, bloody body into the canal. But all she did was give him the one good revenge kick and then grab his arm again and lead him off to wherever they were taking him.

Back in the seclusion of the austere hotel room, Dennis struggled to get online, and I lay back on the stiff mattress in relief. If I hadn't already known I had two herniated disks, I would have sworn both kidneys were failing. Being flat was the single pleasure in my life; the cost of doing anything else was agonizing pain in the center of my back, right above my hips. On my fruitless quest to heal my back, I'd read many accounts of other sufferers who had contemplated suicide, the pain was so endless and severe. I could completely understand this. I'd damaged my back two years earlier while doing a calf workout at the gym. I was taking steroids at the time so that I could achieve the large bubble butt that I knew Dennis so desperately wanted. Now, I'd lost those gym gains and turned myself into a cripple. Annoyingly, he didn't seem aware that my suffering was a direct result of my own mentally ill attempt to please him.

The remainder of our vacation was a bickering failure. I followed alongside Dennis while he walked set-jawed, map in hand, along the winding streets. I stifled my complaints when he located yet another museum, exhibit, or tour for us to attend. Had he suggested we climb down the embankment and into the water to pan for gold, I would have wept in gratitude.

We did not have sex once. When it didn't happen on the first night, some sort of mysterious, unspoken pact formed between us: therefore, it won't happen any of the other nights, either.

I wanted to drink, and I wanted to cry. Instead, I apologized. I was sorry for walking slowly, I was sorry my back hurt and put me in a bad mood, I was sorry I couldn't stand in line without bending over like I'd lost a contact lens on the ground, I was sorry the food grossed me out, I was sorry I couldn't drink casually and enjoy a wine tasting with him, I was sorry we weren't having sex, I was sorry I mentioned the dogs because I missed them, I was sorry I wasn't more fun—"Like you are with your fans." I'd been sober for three years, yet I was still waking up and thinking exactly the same thing: *What's the first thing I need to apologize for today?*

I wondered, *So what's the benefit again? Of being sober?*

Every time I looked at Dennis, all I could see was disgust and resentment. But was that accurate? My instincts seemed to no longer be functioning.

We spent one rainy day inside the hotel room.

"I hope your back feels better after resting today," he said from his seat near the window. Red-faced, he turned the crisp, tall pages of *The New York Times*, not minding at all that the news was over three days old.

By midafternoon, he was opening a bottle of wine for himself. I reminded myself, *I am a free person in the world. I could just do it. There is literally nothing to stop me. I could drink right now.* But I didn't. I finished Anne Frank's diary, feeling entirely awed by it. Awe, I discovered, was my favorite feeling. It was a rare experience, but when it happened, it was like an orgasm for the mind.

I tempted myself again. *Go ahead, grab a wineglass, and pour some for yourself.* I waited, listening. Would I hear a small voice of agreement in my mind, long silenced—*Yes, yes, yes!*—but instead, there was nothing. When I imagined pouring wine into a glass and raising it to my lips for my first sip in three years, I just couldn't work up a craving for this experience. I realized that when I really gave myself actual no-strings-attached permission to drink on vacation, I just didn't want to. The idea, in fact, made me vaguely queasy, as though hearing a rodent scramble from within the wall. But this lack of desire didn't feel like a relief. Rather, it struck me as a form of emptiness.

I thought, *I should feel relieved that, deep down, I really don't want to drink.* But I didn't. I only felt like I'd lost a certain amount of *desire*, and that desire was a bad thing to lose in any capacity, even desire for something you shouldn't have. It seemed stoic to want a drink but not to take it, whereas it was merely sad to not even want one anymore.

On the morning of our flight back to New York, I woke up feeling rejuvenated, exactly the way a person is supposed to feel after a two-week holiday abroad. I was all smiles and no complaints.

"You're happy we're leaving, aren't you?" Dennis asked while he shaved.

"I'm excited to see the dogs," I told him. I could almost smell them.

"Me too," he said, and he smiled so warmly at me that I just about did cry. It was the smallest thing, this kindness in his eyes, but it was everything, and I loved him for it.

"Well, we're only hours away from seeing them," he said.

The way he phrased it; I was thrilled.

We'd recently bought a harness for our year-old French bull-dog, Bentley. He was large, and he pulled, and I worried about his neck, about yanking him back. So we bought him a harness, and then we'd walked up to Fairway, where Dennis waited outside with Bentley, and I went in for goat cheese, frozen peas, corkscrew pasta, and Cokes.

When I came out, he said, "That was fast."

And I didn't say anything. I thought, *I'm surprised it seemed fast.* Because when I got inside, it was mobbed. And every-body seemed to be walking really slowly, and I wanted to whisper something harsh in a couple of people's ears but then stopped and willed myself to calm down. Magically, there was no line at the register. But I didn't say any of this to Dennis. I said, "Yeah."

We walked past the North Face store, and I remembered that I needed flip-flops. Cow, our second Frenchie, was still a puppy and needed to be taken outside constantly, so my feet had blistered from going sockless in my Top-Siders.

"Just one second," I said, and Dennis stood with Bentley and two plastic bags in a pie-shaped slice of sun.

What a day. It was exactly the kind of day that made you say that out loud without feeling cheesy about it. "*What a day!*"

Sunny, midseventies with a breeze. No clouds. Perfect, like the 9/11 day, except for the end-of-the-world part.

I got my flip-flops and joined Dennis on the sidewalk. We headed home, down West End Avenue. The sun was beginning its descent, and I was happy. I was just so simply happy. We had our big beast with us, and the little beast was at home, hopefully not chewing on anything. We were a family, together for three years. I felt *cozy*—that was the word for it. Like there was a log cabin inside my chest instead of a tumor, which was how I used to feel.

"Are you as happy as I am?" I said at the crosswalk. "I mean, are you as happy in this relationship as I am?"

There was more of a pause than you might expect.

Dennis replied, "Not as happy as you, no."

I thought he was kidding me.

His face revealed no spring-snake-in-a-can sort of "Surprise! Just kidding you!" His features remained serious yet strained. And I thought this was part of the ruse. The authenticity of his reply.

"No, really," I said, grinning to prove that I was in on the ruse.

He said, "For the reasons we've talked about before, nothing new. But no. I think you're happier than I am."

And then I understood. He was answering me from his heart, without irony; his guard was down.

I sank through the sidewalk. It was a physical sensation of extraordinary heaviness, as real as though somebody had placed a knapsack filled with river stones on my back. I also became very drowsy, like I wanted to lie down right there at the intersection of Seventy-Second Street and West End Avenue, press my back against the *USA Today* newspaper dispenser, and just sleep.

I said, "Wait," because I needed a do-over. I had the sensation of him speeding forward on an Italian motorcycle, leaving me behind flailing my hands in the air. "What do you mean? Aren't you happy?" The first part came out as a whine; the last part sounded like an accusation.

"I'm happy," he said, sounding annoyed that I was pestering him. "I'm just probably not as happy as you are, that's all."

Was I heartbroken or furious? I didn't know. I did know: that's it. Our relationship could not continue like this, out of balance, unequal.

And as surely as I knew this, I knew something else: *But of course it can.* We can continue to live exactly as we do right now, in a heavy-lidded state of love and unspeakable compromise. Isn't that what people do? Every day? Don't they ache but rename it *tired*?

It made me wonder: Was it even fair to expect the person you're with to be just as happy as you? Furthermore, how could you ever even know for sure? You couldn't, was the truth of it. You could not know this.

As we crossed the street, our grayish-beige high-rise apartment building had all the charm of subsidized housing in Eastern Europe. The sun made me squint, and even though I felt a kindness toward Dennis for being honest, I hated him for admitting he was unhappy. I felt a thrumming panic, like I'd been stranded somewhere on my own but didn't know where or how to get back or even where to go. I suddenly felt completely alone in love.

Last weekend, we'd had a talk, the kind introduced by the words "we need to talk." So we sat on the sofa, and I opened my eyes wide to scare away the impending drowsiness that conflict switches on inside of me, and I looked at him.

"What's up? What do you want to talk about?" I felt sure my face looked open and receptive despite the fact that I actually wanted to cover my ears with my hands like a seven-year-old and run from the room singing, "La la la la la."

"I'm missing some things," he began after clearing his throat.

My mind flashed to items that could have gone missing. His keys? Phone? Socks? But he hadn't misplaced anything. He didn't mean that kind of missing.

Dennis was sad that we didn't do the spontaneous "dating" things that we did back when we were, in fact, dating. Like the time we rented a car and drove to New Jersey of all places to see their version of Shakespeare in the Park. Or the night when we went to the jazz club and I was seeing blue from Viagra. Perhaps he missed the horrible little house I'd owned because it was so much fun to go there and make fun of its faults, never worrying about dust or scuff marks. The thing was, everything he identified as something he missed was from the first couple of months of our relationship. Back when I was trying to be my best self, as opposed to my actual one.

Now we had two dogs, only one of which was housebroken. My career was all consuming. There were two homes, and on weekends, we went to the new house in Northampton, where we tried to keep the grass down, we vacuumed the stairs, went to the supermarket, and bought too much food for two people, hypnotized by the aisles.

I didn't know what to say to him.

"I even miss the pillows you used to have on your bed downtown, when you had your own little apartment."

He missed my pillows? He missed the old me, the one he didn't know yet.

I thought about this conversation in the elevator on the way back to our apartment. Once we were inside, I became angry.

Since he wasn't as happy as I was, I would punish him and make him extra miserable.

"You judge me constantly. You make me feel bad for reading. Jesus fucking Christ. And I let you get away with it. I'm a fucking writer. And I *need* to read. And yet you look down on it in some way, as though there are better things to do. Go outside. See modern dance."

In the kitchen, then, I felt the weight of our incompatibility. A sense that a split was inevitable.

But again, the other side. That people do live like that.

"I love you. I love a lot about our life," he said.

We were being careful not to say things we could not take back.

We put the groceries away. We didn't say anything. Until finally I said, "I shouldn't ask questions if I don't want to know the answers."

He sat at the table. He glanced at the newspaper. He turned the page and cocked his head to study the article. I stood there staring at him, hands poised on my hips. "And," I said, "another thing. I always have to bring things up. You never tell me when something's wrong. I have to drag it out of you."

He nodded, because this was true. He'd admitted it himself. So much for all that therapy.

I thought of something else to say but changed my mind and then decided, screw it. "You're an emotional miser."

His glance returned to the newspaper, and he licked his lips.

Maybe this was unfair, cruel. But it felt true, especially then. Especially because I was so hurt and embarrassed that I was happy. Now, it seemed simpleminded to be happy.

My childhood had been hijacked by drunks, pedophiles, lunatics, and surrealists, so I grew up in a world unrelated to the actual planetary body beneath my feet. I was at the mercy of the off-the-rails adults around me. The upside was, I became determined as an adult to do what *I* wanted: become an author, get published, become sober, get love.

Security and love, these were the two things I did not feel as a child, so I chased after them now, sometimes bumping into things and knocking them down in the process. I was an emotional Great Dane, hugely needy and clumsy.

Dennis read the paper, and I made updates to my Web site. No sense in trying to talk more about this when he'd shut down, tuning me out.

I let the puppy out of his crate. He peed on the newspaper, ideal. And then he and Bentley mouthed each other, rolled, frolicked, snapped, and chased each other around the apartment.

Dennis had moved to the sofa and was still reading the paper.

I said, "This morning, I wanted to read. Remember we talked about it last night, how I haven't been reading enough? So, this morning I was going to read, and that's when you decided to clean."

Dennis looked up at me as I spoke but then turned his face away from me, indignant. This gesture infuriated me.

"You were dragging that fucking vacuum all over the place, but especially near the bed where I was trying to start a new book. I wanted something, and you wouldn't give it to me. I wanted one morning to read, but you don't approve of reading on sunny days, so you punished me for it."

Today, I felt like letting nothing go.

I had been naïve. I had chosen to believe something for both of us. I believed that my own hope was enough for two. That because I was so happy with the idea of us, this of course meant he must be, too.

I was terrified. What if we split? What if this was the end?

I was pushing like I was trying to make it the end, but that's not what I wanted.

Fuck.

Why couldn't we just talk about this shit?

I stomped away and went back to the dining room table where my laptop sat. Dennis shut down when there was a conflict, and I was the opposite: I had to talk about it. It was unbearable not to. His silence then became this thing I had to break apart with my words. I hated the sound of my own voice when I was like this.

Dennis just sat there, silently turning the pages as though this were the most normal thing in the world, this distance between us, this lopsided communication.

Was it normal?

Or was this a base-level problem, a foundation issue? When you added the sex in, when you considered that we barely had any, it seemed sad.

I knew that he would get up at ten or eleven to make dinner, but by then, it would be too late. And I would say, "I'm not going to eat anything this late. Don't bother if it's for me. Only cook if you want it."

He showed his love for me by cooking. I bought ingredients, and he was not going to cook until late. He was going to withhold this. I knew him and knew this is what he would do.

Perhaps I am wrong and he will not play this game, I thought. *Perhaps I am inventing things.*

Was I insane? Or was the window suddenly clean? It made me crazy not to know. And I was still so drowsy.

I studied him sitting there, ignoring me. I wanted to say

something hurtful or sharp or pointed. I wanted to say something that could ease the tension, but I also wanted it to build and build. I always had to be the one who said, "Is something wrong?" Because if I didn't say it, it didn't get said.

So should I say something now? Or just let him read, let things go on as they are. Make no move to hurt, no move to repair. Just go and drift, together, or apart.

We did not speak to each other the rest of the night. We went to bed. He made no attempt to cook, so we had nothing for dinner. I woke up in the night and ate four chocolates.

The puppy woke me at seven thirty, though I think Dennis had gotten up earlier, taken care of him, and put him back in his crate. Dennis woke up again, and while he took Bentley outside, I fed the tiny puppy and tried to get him to poop on his newspapers. When they returned, we let the dogs play.

Dennis went back to bed. We said nothing to each other. Not even "Good morning."

Last night on the way back from the grocery store, I'd been so happy. The thing I'd always been chasing, it seemed like maybe I'd finally caught up with it. Of course, Dennis had to feel it, too. How could he not? This seventy-five degrees and cloudless content? *Are you so, so happy, too?*

"Not as happy as you."

With those words, we became incompatible. Two people, not just one, not as happy as they could be in the relationship.

I could have moved to him, said something, corrected this before it got worse. But I knew that would not happen.

———

Bentley vomited on the rug three times. He was clingy, molding his body to fit my calves, tucking into, against, the bone. He went from Dennis on the bed back over to me on the couch. He threw up white foam as though he'd been eating pieces of the ocean.

We were halfway through day two of our standoff when we finally talked.

I am insecure and short-circuit when my security is threatened. I admitted this. But then I managed to hurt him by telling him he was judgmental every day. He asked for examples, evidence, but the drowsy feeling came.

The thing was, I felt he was so judgmental about almost everything that it was difficult to pluck a mere example out of the air to serve as evidence. It was like trying to prove we were in the midst of a sunny day. "Well, we just are. I mean, *look*."

We talked but did not resolve. Things felt awkward but not awful. And like somebody who decides to leave the moldy bread in the refrigerator just to see what will eventually happen, I decided, fine.

I wouldn't be the happier one anymore.

We moved through this conflict the way one drives through suddenly torrential and frightening rain: feeling that a crash was imminent but with an unspoken agreement to say nothing at all.

We moved out of Dennis's Upper West Side apartment

and into the house we'd built in Massachusetts, where construction was mostly complete. I was astonished by the way the formally *intolerable* was transmogrified into the merely mundane.

In a way, it was as though the fight that had begun on the sidewalk outside the supermarket never really ended. It merely continued into another state and extended for years. The difference was, we were no longer cooped up together in a studio apartment. We had three floors filled with distractions to keep us divided. It was fascinating how quickly and permanently we settled into a daily routine with so much physical space between us: I worked downstairs; Dennis settled into the room he created as an office upstairs. We e-mailed each other during the day, he cooked at night while I remained on my laptop, and then we ate together at midnight.

The man who bought Dennis's New York apartment had reminded me of Dennis somehow. He was exceedingly jovial in almost exactly the same indiscriminate way, and I wondered if he and Dennis would become friends. I was surprised when Dennis was chilly with him.

I called Christopher every day and no longer thought of him as just my agent but my best friend. Though even more than this, really, because he was the only person in the world that I liked. Because he'd read every word I'd ever written about myself, he already knew exactly how horrible I was and, still, he took my calls.

I ordered him a gift from late-night home shopping TV and had it sent without a card or any return address, and he guessed it was from me right away.

"But how did you know?" I demanded to know.

He laughed into the phone. "Because who else in the world would send me a Sheena Easton doll? I mean, she's porcelain and permanently on her knees, always *just about* to give a blow job; she has wings!"

Dennis pointed at the pipe sticking out of the wall in the corner of the garage and frowned. "I worry this sink will feel crammed stuck in the corner like that. I wonder if we should have moved it more toward the center."

But of course we'd had this conversation: the sink could *not* be moved into the center of the garage's rear wall because on the other side of that wall was the yellow TV room, and he knew this.

This was Dennis's dream sink. It would allow him to in-dulge his fetish: washing out the rags he would use to wash our cars and buff them to a diamond finish. The builder in-stalled the plumbing for the sink in the only place that made sense: tucked into the corner, out of the way of the counters he was also going to install.

We had been standing in the still-incomplete garage for close to forty minutes, Dennis tracing his fingers over the barn-board wainscoting he had installed. Soon there would be shelving that ran along the walls beginning midway and continuing up to the ceiling. Instead of fluorescent lights, we'd installed old hanging schoolhouse lanterns. The curtains were being sewn as we stood there and would be hung the following week. This garage was nicer than most apartments

I'd lived in in Manhattan. But I lacked the patience to stand in it and second-guess the location of the sink.

Somebody told us, "Building a house together is a real test of a relationship. If you can survive that, you can survive anything." I interpreted this as, building the house would be the single and largest test of our relationship ever, and once it's over, you can relax and be happy, finally.

I told Dennis, "You know, it's gonna be fine. There's gonna be like three inches between the sink and the wall, so I think we'll be okay."

Dennis said, "Yeah, that's true. There will be those three inches."

So, these were my problems now. Will my new garage sink feel crammed into the corner, or would those three inches give it some breathing room? My new sink, in my new climate-controlled garage, in my new luxury cottage, with copper rain gutters and native stone floors. These were my concerns now. My own life felt utterly unfamiliar to me. Distant and pristine, as though belonging to somebody else. As I stood in the garage I thought, *This must be what happy feels like.*

I had a career that involved sitting in a comfortable chair and which provided me with enough free time to dress the dogs in T-shirts every day and laugh at them. I'd been a store detective, Ground Round waiter, and advertising copywriter, so I knew it really did not get better than this. Furthermore, I did not have a fatal illness, and I was certain baldness would be cured in my lifetime.

As far as I could see, my life now was the opposite of my

chaotic, off-the-rails childhood or my drunken twenties in New York.

And yet there were certain details in my new life that seemed suspect upon closer inspection. Like the fact that Dennis and I had built this house in the same town where I was raised.

We would be living on a cul-de-sac. And while many New Yorkers sneer at stores like Target and Walmart, I was openly thrilled to be living within a few miles of both. I already had my pet superstore discount card.

When this eco-friendly, SUV-hating college town was in an uprising over the local buffalo farm being sold and developed into a Lowe's home improvement store, I was ready to picket. "YOU CAN'T FIX A SINK WITH A BUFFALO!!! IN WITH LOWE'S!!!" I looked at the pristine Hadley farmland and could think of nothing more beautiful than replacing those trees along the borders of the fields with a parking lot for seventeen hundred cars.

I wanted a "normal" suburban childhood, and now I was going to have it, thirty years later. And I was going to have it in a plastic bag with a logo stamped on the front, along with a coupon to save 5 percent next time.

This was a college town filled with extremely well-educated people who drove Volvos and wore clothing made from sustainable fibers. It had always been this way. And while there were several McMansions in the area, I was sure that in time, some local environmentalist group would burn them to the ground.

Crime in this town was mostly college kids doing vile college things involving beer, condoms, and mailboxes.

We left the garage and climbed back into the car. As we drove down the street, I was thinking about how happy I would soon be, here in this town I kind of loathed but with my stable and normal mate imported directly from the Upper West Side. I saw flashing blue lights in the rearview mirror.

"God fucking damn it," Dennis said, looking in the rearview mirror. "Shit."

He eased the car over to the side and threw it into park. He dropped his hands in his lap and then quickly reached for the glove compartment.

"Here, we need the registration," he said.

It didn't seem that we were going all that fast.

A young, beefy cop appeared at the driver-side window and said the usual, "License and registration, please."

Dennis passed these to the cop, who then walked back to his cruiser.

As we sat, Dennis fumed. "I was not speeding. This is just bullshit. This is just . . ."

I warned him, "Whatever you do, don't piss him off. Don't get him mad. Or it'll just be worse."

Dennis seemed to be one of those people who had decades of rage simmering below the surface, masked by a smile.

The cop returned and passed the documents back to Dennis. He said, "Do you know how fast you were going?"

Dennis replied, "I think I was going fifty."

The cop said, "Did you see the speed limit sign?"

Dennis told him, "Well, it was fifty-five back there. And then I think it changed to forty-five."

The cop said, "You were going fifty-four miles per hour. And the speed limit was forty. You may not have seen the sign. But it was there."

Then the cop noticed something on our dashboard: a small green indication lamp. He walked around to the front of the vehicle and then returned. "It's illegal to use fog lights when it's not foggy."

It was currently six degrees below zero in western Massachusetts, and we drove with fog lights because there were large, flat sheets of ice on the road. They were easy to miss. Unless you had on the fog lights and could see them.

The cop wrote out a ticket and passed it to Dennis. Then he returned to his car. The ticket was for $175, including $40 for the fog lights. As we pulled out, the cop followed behind us.

Dennis kept checking his rearview mirror. "That fucker is following us," he said. "To make sure we don't speed." And he pulled into the parking lot of a convenience store.

The cop drove on by. And we sat there for a moment. Dennis was fuming. "There was no fucking sign. I was going fifty-four. The speed limit was just fifty-five. I saw *that* sign. What the fuck?"

He said, "I'm going to fight this ticket. That was some sort of trap. Who do they think they're pulling over? That road is all local residents going home from work."

I knew he wouldn't fight it, because he was speeding, if only just a little. And what sort of case is that? But the fog lights thing. That's bullshit. That's not a ticket for fog lights; that's a ticket for two fags from Manhattan in a black Range Rover.

After the speeding and fog lamp ticket, we became aware of just how many cops patrolled this small New England college town where we were about to live, and it was a little alarming.

"Look at that," Dennis said the following night as we approached the local strip mall. "Will you just take a good look at that." He made a *tsk* sound and shook his head from side to side. A cop had pulled over a minivan. Peering in the window as we drove by, I saw it was an ordinary woman, probably a mother.

Dennis was still livid from his previous brush with law enforcement, so he was especially compassionate toward her. "Yeah, right. There are people who want to fly planes into our nuclear power plants and dump poison in our reservoirs, and these fat-assed college-town cops have nothing better to do than pull over some soccer mom in a blue minivan. Bullshit."

I laughed, but then when I looked at his face, I saw he was enraged. He wasn't being funny; he was being borderline personality disorder-ish.

But then? Less than two miles down the street, we saw *another* cop, this one speeding in the opposite direction. I assumed he was driving to the scene to assist the other cop with the dangerous tampon user.

Until we could move into our new house the following week, we were living in a local motel that we called the Roach Motel. It was the sort of motel where the carpets were composed of equal parts nylon fiber and dried bodily fluids. We stayed there because it was one of the few places in the area that would accept our two dogs.

The dogs had come to accept the Roach Motel as home and playpen. There were two full-sized beds in the room with only a slender nightstand between them, so the dogs were able to leap from one bed to the other. They chased each other this way, back and forth between the beds. It was as if this bit of canine acrobatics was something programmed into their genetic code.

We reached the Roach Motel and slid into the parking space directly in front of our door. The motel was actually sort of charming red brick with twenty rooms, though uncared for. But if a couple of gays were to buy the place, redecorate it, and jack the prices up and out of the range of keg-crazed frat boys with hard-ons and roofies, it'd be a nice place.

Inside the room, I grabbed my laptop and peeled back the covers. We needed to use all four flat foam pillows on our one bed.

Immediately, I noticed the smell of cologne wafting up from the sheets. I leaned in close and saw crinkly red pubic hairs. Definitely not hairs from either of us.

Luckily, the sheets on the opposite bed were clean. So I switched them around and then turned on HGTV to watch the downscale decorating shows that Dennis found so amusing. In some rear compartment of my mind, I realized I kind of liked living in the semicharming, semigross motel room and almost dreaded moving into our cedar-shingled, plaster-walled dream home.

At eleven, we drove to Chili's to pick up our takeout order. On the way back, Dennis decided to stop into the convenience store to get some milk. But when we pulled up to the curb in front of the place, we noticed a trio of suspicious youths. What made them suspicious was that they had mullets. Programmed by years of living in Manhattan, I immediately suspected that these weren't ordinary college kids but unsavory white trash from the nearby slum town of Holyoke. Even-staid Dennis was on alert.

"That looks a little weird, doesn't it?" he said.

"Yes, it does," I agreed. "I think they're probably about to go in that store and rob it. I wouldn't go in, seriously. They could easily have guns. This is bad. Look at their hair."

Dennis wasn't paranoid the way I was. But these were undeniably scummy kids. We drove away.

Then Dennis happened to glance in the rearview mirror and saw that the little psychopaths had actually walked into the center of the street and were now watching us as we drove away. So maybe I wasn't so paranoid after all. Maybe I was just fucking savvy.

The motel was just around the corner from the store and the hoodlums. If we turned into the driveway, they would definitely see us. And even if they hadn't intended to hold up the store and shoot the clerk in the head, now we'd insulted them by driving away at the mere sight of them. So surely they would teach us a lesson and shuffle over to the motel parking lot, find our car, and smash all the windows with large rocks. They might even try to pry their way inside the room and kill our dogs.

My therapist back in New York told me that one of my problems is that I create these elaborate fantasies—always of disaster—and then my emotional response engages as though it's actually happening. In other words, because I imagine all these horrible things happening at all times, the stress on my body is so bad, they might as well just be happening. The problem is, so many horrible things have actually happened to me that it's hard for me to buy this "It's all in your head" bullshit.

I told Dennis I was worried the thugs were going to break into the room and kill the dogs, so instead of turning into the driveway, he made a left onto a side street.

That's where we saw a police cruiser, slowly driving along the street perpendicular to ours, about one hundred feet away. Seeing us, the police cruiser drifted to a stop.

Now, we drove into one of the residential driveways and then backed out. We turned around. Something perfectly normal. And while it was late, it wasn't so late. Didn't people in the suburbs drive after 10:00 P.M.?

We cruised back to the traffic light and made a right. Safe now from the eyes of the eventual inmates, we drove up to our motel room door and parked.

"You just watch," Dennis said, "that fucking cop is going to drive right past us now."

And sure enough, he did.

The next morning, we saw three police cruisers in the three miles between the Roach Motel and our house. So, basically, one cop per mile.

"This is just unbelievable," I said. Somewhere deep in my bones, I had known all along that moving back to this town had been a terrible mistake. My first childhood had been horrible enough; why would I even want a second chance in the same fucking town?

We came across a cop who had pulled over an old man

in a pickup truck. An old man! In a pickup truck! *These cops should be hunting down those kids from last night,* I thought. They should be slamming them to the ground and beating them with nightsticks, not ticketing onion-growing seniors. I thought, *We could have been killed last night. Those kids should be in handcuffs.*

That evening in the room over a dinner of pizza from Joe's in Northampton, I went online to research these Amherst cops. What I found was an interesting local Web site that displayed an activity log from the Amherst Police Department.

Here, under the heading "Suspicious Activity," I noticed a number of curious entries.

The first stated, "Four individuals inside copy center turned out to be employees." To make sure I'd read it correctly, I read it again.

Exactly what were they implying?

Wasn't it likely that if there were four people inside a copy shop, at least some of them would work there? Also, they still had copy shops?

The next item on the list was worse. "People in white van turned out to be waiting for man walking dog."

Dennis was in the bathroom washing his hands, and I called him over.

"You gotta take a look at this!" I hollered.

He came over to the bed drying his hands on a bleach-scented towel. I turned the laptop around so the screen faced him.

"Check it out. Second line from the top. Or fuck it, read the top one, too."

I watched him scan the page and saw his eyebrows pop up in recognition. "Oh, you've got to be kidding me. They're hunting down people who are out walking their dogs now?"

"That is a little weird, isn't it?" I said.

I was a little worried about this. Maybe more than a little worried. After all, we might be staying in a motel now, guests of the town, but in just a few days, we'd be living here. This would be our hometown.

If they were going after copy shop employees for just being copy shop employees, I would *for sure* be put behind bars.

If you can think of a suspicious activity, chances are good it's something I engage in unwittingly every day. Nearly everything about me is suspicious: I twitch my shoulders when I walk (plastic explosives strapped to my body?), I check my pockets constantly (carrying concealed weapon?), I tend to stare into people's windows when I walk past their houses (sexual predator?).

At this rate, we wouldn't be settled a week before my face would be plastered on the front of the local newspaper under the headline NEW AMHERST RESIDENT NABBED IN PIZZA SLICE INCIDENT.

Dennis saw another one. "Look here. It says, 'Man reported standing near bushes no longer there when police arrive.' Did you get that? Somebody reported a man standing near bushes."

I could see the scene in my mind: a forty-seven-year-old professor of semiotics at Amherst College, standing just off the town common near a bush. He's thinking, *Wait a minute. What did Ann want me to pick up on the way home? Apple cider donuts?* So he's standing there, and then one of the intolerant

Amherst locals, clearly brainwashed by the local law enforcement agency, saw this and panicked. "Who is that man? Why is he standing there? Who just stands in place without moving? Maybe that goes over okay in Sherman Oaks, California, but it's sure not okay here. I'm calling nine-one-one."

Dennis and I looked at each other. "This isn't good," he said. "There's an awful lot of *suspicious activity* on this page, and none of it looks very suspicious to me."

"Holy shit," I said. "We're moving into a police state. This is like an Eastern Bloc country in World War II." How long, I could only wonder, would it be before a bronze statue of Stalin was erected on the town commons, directly opposite the Lord Jeffery Inn? And didn't some of the older UMASS dorms look very much like upscale New England concentration camp buildings? Surely, they would be easy to retrofit. Perhaps a plan was already in place. And who'd be the first inside the gas chambers? Absolutely, the insufferable gay guys from New York.

I couldn't continue thinking this way. I had to see the flip side. I said to Dennis, "But the great thing is that there's just not much crime here. Just students screwing off. Maybe they have a couple of robberies now and then, but that's it."

"Well, yeah," Dennis said. "Of course there's no crime. The citizens are too terrified to make a move. I bet three-quarters of the population don't leave their houses. I mean, look at this log." He pointed to another entry. "Says here that police approached a man on a path. And it turned out the man was waiting for his friend." He was crazed. "This is just unbelievable. They're nabbing *friends*. On *paths*."

One would think they'd have better things to do. But

then, maybe these are the better things, and they're doing them. Maybe now, you do have to stop the mom in the minivan and the man on the path waiting for his friend. I expect you do. The alternative—an "Anything goes!" police department—would not do.

In the city now, you had to expect the plane to fly into the building, the subway to explode. But in the country, you didn't have to expect this yet.

I decided it was good that the area was so heavily policed. I wasn't planning on ever leaving the house, anyway, since I hated small towns and nature and political correctness and pretty much everything that existed outside of New York City where, it was beginning to sink in, I actually no longer lived.

Dennis continued to drive into Manhattan on a regular basis to see his therapist, and Wednesday was the night Dennis's therapist decided would be our scheduled sex night. Because if we didn't agree on a time and make a firm commitment, things would continue as they were, meaning no sex ever. I actually would have preferred this but of course couldn't feel that way, so I said I thought that Wednesday sex was a good idea, very smart.

"We don't have to come or get hard, either. But we have to try," he said.

Which was like the captain of the swim team saying, "Just don't drown and you'll be a winner!" The therapist had set our bar extremely low, and still, I wasn't sure I could meet it.

I *had* been trying. I had a shelf of mortifying sexual-health books to prove it. One, *Anal Pleasures*, grossed me out so much I had to keep it turned around so the spine faced the wall. And other books, mostly on the subject of childhood sexual assault.

So we were about to have sex, but it felt like I was about to have some sort of oral surgery where I would not be allowed to go under general anesthesia and must also watch the procedure—which would certainly involve long needles and a great amount of blood—on video screens installed in the ceiling.

I'd known all day that we would have sex that night, and I had been dreading the prospect.

He was closing the shades. I was glad for this. I didn't want the neighbors to witness the spectacle of my own miserable failure.

It was time.

We stood facing each other and kissed. His hand went to my cool, soft cock, and mine went to his.

"I want you to be turned on," he said.

With a chill, I recalled that Mitch had spoken almost exactly these same words to me so many years ago. I was living my life adhering to the exact definition of insanity: when a behavior failed, I just kept doing it over and over, expecting a different result.

Dennis wanted me to be turned on, and I couldn't tell him that was not going to happen, because I refused to believe this myself.

We moved to the bed. I wanted nothing more than to turn onto my side and curl up.

"Are you okay?" he asked.

I said, "Yeah."

I was not okay. The mere touch of his hand filled me with unaccountable fury instead of passion. I felt like, *I don't belong here.*

A small and unfamiliar voice, a psychological interloper told me, *This is called* instinct. *You should trust this.*

Naturally, I ignored the voice. Because I did not recognize it as instinct but rather assumed it was my unhealthy inner addict. My drinking voice. I cannot trust any voice inside my head unless I am wearing earbuds.

We were a couple.

Why could we not be lovers?

I was so frustrated and confused. I knew Dennis was, too. I thought, *This cannot be because I was molested as a boy.* What was it? Why was I so disconnected when we tried to have sex? I then thought, *I wish I could call Christopher and ask his advice.*

The thought stunned me.

I should not be thinking about my literary agent on the one night during the week Dennis's therapist said we should be practicing having sex.

And in an instant, I saw the problem: I loved somebody else.

My life was crumbling away from me, like I forgot to mix the glue in with the substrate. Hour by literal hour, Dennis and I disengaged. We had managed to create two separate rooms on two separate floors within the space of one queen-sized bed. I found I couldn't fall asleep until he was snoring. Only then was sleep possible, but it only arrived after a great deal of ceiling-watching. I started sleeping on top of the covers, almost like I was expecting to flee in the middle of the night.

But I do fall asleep, and there he is yet again: the Jeep Guy. Only, where's the Jeep? This time, we're together in a low-riding motorboat of some primitive kind, crawling through a flooded bayou of Louisiana. I am terrifyingly aware that we have one skimpy outboard motor and a very thin wall of aluminum between us and whatever is down there knocking and sliding around the bottom of the boat. The recurring dream has brought a sense of foreboding with it this time.

But my dusty-armed lifeguard of a guy is up front, and he's navigating, and he is so not worried at all.

My legs stretch out in front of me as I hold on to the outboard motor stick steering thing. I peer over the right side, horrified to see that the copperhead- and alligator-infested water is just inches below the rim of the boat. I feel the sort of panic that stretches out in dreams, a suffocating sense of impossibility. But Jeep Guy is smiling and pointing to a red neon sign along the shore with a dock and slips for boats.

"That's the place," he says, nodding in the direction of the sign. "This is where it ends."

Good, I think, finally. Then in a bloom of panic: *Wait. Where what ends?*

The aroma of french fries and vinegar reaches me, and my relief is instantaneous. Next comes the awareness that nothing has ever gone wrong with this rugged guy, and in fact, he is the star of my best dreams, the only ones I could ever remember long enough to tell someone about. But the mountain is gone, and he's leading me through a swamp that smells like french fries and feels like the end. In the boat, I am afraid to love because the water level is so high that I know we'll sink. We don't. But I was sure we would.

In my other Jeep Guy dreams, the only thing I'd ever been sure of was him. And I didn't even know his name. More worrisome, I didn't even know if he thought I was attractive.

When I awoke, it felt like my private dream life had been savagely violated and destroyed. I had now real doubts. Jeep Guy had never said he loved me. Dennis said he loved me only when I pestered him, and after he said it, I suspected him of lying.

I had a heartbreaking sense that there would be no more Jeep Guy dreams.

My doctor called me. He and I had become friends. I called him by his first name, he showed me his vacation shots, and we talked about his love life. If he didn't actually wear one of those starched white jackets, I might have forgotten he was even a physician, let alone mine. We'd moved beyond the strict "doctor/patient" relationship. I introduced him to range-finder photography, and he introduced me to meth-amphetamine.

Oddly enough, it did seem like we were both better off.

Peter had gotten to know me. I had long ago stopped playing Happy and Well-Adjusted Guy with him. So he'd witnessed firsthand the authentic bus out of control that is me, the frantic-with-stress, prone-to-fury, swinging-instantly-into-grief me.

Nine months after he became my doctor, he called. "Do you have a minute?"

Obviously, when your doctor phones in the middle of an afternoon and asks if you have a minute, pretty much the next thing you need to do is go casket shopping.

"Yeah, what's going on?"

He said, "I have suspected this from the beginning, but I really needed to know you better before I was sure. I really think you have ADD—or ADHD, as it's called now." He added, "But without the hyperactivity component."

"Isn't that a kid thing?" I asked. I associated ADD with preposterously annoying, constantly shrieking and clawing children running around loose in stores. The kids who streak past you screaming gibberish, smearing themselves all over the world, and all you can think is, *Just die.*

"Adults can have it, too," he said. "And you need meds."

So he put me on Adderall. Which is the sleek, postmodern name for basically the same pills those girls were taking in *Valley of the Dolls.*

After listing all the reasons why I needed to be medicated, not the least of which was the fact that I asked him questions like "Wait, what were we just talking about?" he wrote a prescription and told me he wanted to hear from me frequently. He said it could take time to settle on the right dose, so he was going to start me low.

As I swallowed the first pill, I thought, *I can't believe I have a mental condition that has to be treated with fucking dolls.*

I didn't notice much of a change the first day, because an hour after taking the first pill, I could barely keep my eyes open. College students took this shit to help them study? It made me feel like I had been born in California and home-schooled by a stoner mom and a surfer dad.

I was in bed by nine.

On the second day, I noticed a change. My sense of smell had been activated beyond all reason or belief. Everything was overwhelming. The stink of paper. The fumes from an orange. And oh my fucking God, I very nearly began to cry when out of sheer olfactory exhaustion I collapsed on the bed and buried my face in the pillows. My down pillows that were handmade by factory-working moms in Minnesota? They stank like decomposing ducks, as if I went out in the middle of the night looking for the foulest fowl I could find by the side of the road and then scraped it up and laid my head on it.

The only mental effect I had observed was the sensation, however vague, that somebody had actually reached gloved fingers into my skull and was gripping my brain and rearranging it. Just a little. When I stood up, the world appeared somewhat lopsided. When I sat down to write a note to myself, I stared at the blinking cursor and thought, *Wait, is that what music is?*

On the one hand, I was happy to have a proper diagnosis. Aside from a trust fund and a royal title, that was really the only thing I'd ever wanted in life. On the other hand, I was offended to learn that my brain was defective. Or, I suppose I should say, "differently abled."

One thing I was *not* was surprised. Four generations of

manic depression on my mother's side of the family. Three of autism on my father's. Drug addict uncles, a pyromaniac cousin, a couple of schizophrenics and suicides, several flesh-and-blood geniuses, and a pecan farmer. You just cannot mix those raw ingredients together and then stick them inside my mother to simmer for nine months and expect something normal to come out. It's a wonder I wasn't born with a set of horns.

What did kind of amaze me, though, was that there was a pill. All through life, everybody was always telling me, "Don't just think your problems can be solved by popping a pill." But according to my doctor, mine would be. I read the clinical presentation of ADHD in the *Physicians' Desk Reference*, a list of symptoms that read like the "About the Author" page on the back of my book. I actually copied and pasted the whole thing into an e-mail and sent it to Christopher. He wrote back, "Wow. Did you write this yourself?"

By the second week, I was still living in the 3-D World of Smell Molecules. And because Adderall truly did enable me to focus on one thing only, I could think of absolutely nothing else. My doctor promised that this was just a side effect that would pass. But every few hours, I would think, *I am seriously not going to make it. I don't think I can have a fixed brain if it comes with a bionic nose.*

My diet ginger ale also tasted like cheap chemicals. It was just . . . junky. Of course, that's exactly what diet ginger ale is: cheap, junky chemicals in a polyethylene terephthalate container with a screw top. Seeing the truth about something, even though it's stinky and unpleasant, can hardly be considered a side effect.

For as long as I could remember, the first thing I felt when I woke up in the morning was panic. This was followed by dread. When I was little, the dread was related to school. As an adult, the dread was of the free-agent variety. It showed up whenever and wherever and was not particularly attached to anything specific.

The other thing about my brain was that there had always been something circular and repetitive about it. From compulsive tics to endless cycles of worry, worry, worry. I'd always been able to do a great many things, but most of them were missing large chunks and had unfinished edges. It was not just a difficulty in completing tasks but a difficulty in knowing which tasks to even begin.

The drug was doing something not just to my brain but to my mind. I was beginning to have a sensation or emotion I had never felt before. Yet the newness of it made it difficult for me to name.

I sat on the leather chair at my desk, which stank furiously like a dead cow, and considered this feeling. I finally arrived at this: I felt okay. Not a feeling of general well-being. Not a boost in my mood and not any kind of euphoria, like I'd experienced before with painkillers like Vicodin, which was just a delightful pill. What I felt wasn't so much an addition as a subtraction. There was a sense of relief. Not numb, like a zombie. But like "things" had stopped trying to swarm and gather around me and press against me.

I felt less like my mind was spraying out in all directions at once.

After three weeks, I wanted to take a shish kebab skewer and punch it through my nose and into my brain to pop my olfactory nerve. It was as if my brain was breaking down life's aromas into their individual scent components.

I could smell something sour and musky in rubber, also something oily. My belt smelled like spoiled meat, and I wondered how anybody could even wear one and if I'd ever be able to again. From the bedroom on the third floor of our house, I could smell the reeking chemical stink of a volleyball on a shelf in a distant corner of the basement.

One night as I lay in bed, I felt not the dulling of the crushing pressures, not the release from obsessive worry that I would hope from the pills, but rather an intensified kind of worry, a throbbing, focused, and much more tangible dread. Did Dennis actually love me? Did he even like me? Or was it merely an act of tolerance? As my mind stopped racing, my attention seemed to settle over the state of my relationship.

I left our bed and went upstairs to his office and turned on the light, and I felt a tightness spread from the top of my chest, up my neck, and into my face. I looked at his desk chair, the yellow Post-it notes stuck to the top edge of his laptop screen. The envelopes, papers, bills—all his work up there—were organized, laid out, and arranged with meticulous care.

It felt like there was a ghost or a spirit in the room, as though the arrangement of the yellow Post-it notes, the crisply ordered documents stacked flush on the desk, the overwhelming neatness of the office, of the room where Dennis spent all his waking life: it was all so horribly sad.

I pictured his face, and I knew at once what I had been refusing to know. I wanted to touch the space bar, awaken his laptop, and read his e-mail. I wanted to search for a message, "To: New Person, From: Dennis. Dear New Person, When can I see you again? It is nearly over with the Broken Guy."

I backed away from his computer and looked instead at the photographs, mostly of me, on his bookshelf.

Dennis's level, even smile made him look like what, exactly? Like he was trying, like he was doing his best to be happy, because I was pointing a camera at him and our relationship was new and I had dazzling ideas about us as a couple that I pitched, ever the ad guy.

In another photo, I am wearing a baseball cap. We were in Central Park that morning. It was a Sunday. My first book had been published, and there would be another; I had such fierce optimism and determination in my eyes, unmistakable: the phoenix rising once more from the ashes. Or the ruthlessly ambitious vessel of need. Which one was it? I leaned in closer. Looking at those eight-year-old pictures of myself, I saw such hope in my eyes.

Eye on the prize.

I realized I was the goal, achieved. I was what that guy in the photograph wanted to be. The relationship did last. We did build a life together and a home. I did publish a book, and damn, I even got pretty well famous, as far as authors go.

Then that old hollow feeling returned, the one that used to make me feel like I was filled with echoes and wind, the light at dusk in a living room where all the bulbs have burned out and the shadows are crawling in. I felt something tear inside my mind, a splitting, not unlike how my mother would describe her own psychotic breaks after the fact. But this tear was not explosive; it was surgical, precise. The ripping of a scrim.

It was the revealing of clarity, shimmering jewellike in the center of my mind.

I was awakened.

My heart was broken.

I knew, too, so was Dennis's.

I turned off the light, quietly padded downstairs, and crawled back into bed. I turned on my side and pressed my body up against Dennis, and he moved in his sleep to meet me, chest to back, his arm over mine.

I spoke. "This is how we used to sleep, remember? Before the dogs?"

He made a sleepy sound.

And I said, "Do you still love me?"

And he replied, "I still love you."

And in exactly the same way that my nose now dissected my morning coffee into the fat of the fatty milk, the sour note of alkaline, an almost chocolatey nut and chlorine in the water, I heard the truth that thrummed in frequency with the tone in his voice.

Half-asleep, he'd replied, "Yes, I still love you."

But what he'd actually *said* was, "No, I do not."

Adderall had cleared the cobwebs from my mind. The very cobwebs upon which I'd built my life.

For two nights in a row, Dennis worked on the "bookkeeping" in his office until almost four in the morning. I only thought to ask him about it when I realized he looked like a meth addict; strung out and sweaty and just bad.

"There's a discrepancy, and I've got to locate it," he said.

"With what?" I asked. "Where is it? What are you talking about?"

"It's in the checking account. My calculations don't match the bank's."

I felt like I could possibly freak out over this. We would be indicted on fraud charges and led away in handcuffs to serve prison sentences in separate facilities.

"How much is it off?"

He told me it was less than ten cents but that it was important to locate the source of the miscalculation.

I experienced a Shelley Duvall in *The Shining* moment, where she reads Jack's novel in progress and it's hundreds of pages filled with the same text: *All work and no play makes Jack a dull boy.*

I said, "Ten cents. You've been locked away up here for two days going insane over a dime? That's madness, Dennis."

This had the undesired effect of making him angry. I wanted to make him understand: your time is more valuable; your life is more valuable. But it was like opposing somebody's religion. A transformation of thought was just not within the realm of possibility.

As I looked at him hunched over his desk looking like a man in his late sixties, I thought, *I'm terrible for him. If this is the result of almost a decade together, this is proof that we don't work.*

I'd been in enough relationships with completely wrong people to recognize when I'd done it once again.

I left Dennis in his office and walked downstairs. I looked out the darkening window at the oak trees in the backyard, silhouettes against the fading sky. I thought of oak barrels, slowly aging scotch, the flammable feeling in the back of the throat when you take the first drink after a long, long dry spell.

I opened the refrigerator and took out a Diet Coke.

How the fuck did I get here? I thought. If I was going to be completely sober for the rest of my life, if I couldn't even have one drink at the end of a long and brittle day, then the life I lived needed to be a life from which I did not seek escape.

I went into my office and dashed off an e-mail to Christopher. "Trick question: if your checkbook was out of balance by ten cents, would you spend two nights searching for the error?"

He wrote back in five minutes. "Trick reply: no."

His e-mails always made me laugh, even when they were only three words.

Nonetheless, I was in the mood to drink every bottle in the glass-front wine refrigerator we'd installed under the oiled soapstone counter in the living room. I hated my life. It was just exactly that simple.

Splitting the atom. This is what I had to do. As a couple, we had been reduced to what could be reduced no more. All that remained was to split the universe wide open.

I don't like the word *divorce*, because it tells me nothing. "They're divorced" leaves me wondering if this is what they both wanted and if now they are good, no-longer-married friends who go see live music together and ask each other why it was never this easy as a couple. Or had unhappiness in one of them metastasized over the years until just watching him chew a piece of Trident gum made her grit her teeth in hatred? Or was there a betrayal, and did one spouse want to work through the hurt and anger but the other wanted nothing more to do with the marriage? That was my problem with the word.

With death, however, you may not know how or when, but none of that really matters too terribly much in the end, because death means dead and dead means nothing, gone, no more. I have lost people both ways. Through murky, ill-defined divorce and through the sledgehammer that is death.

Death was easier.

No matter how much ambiguity I still felt about this man, despite moments or sometimes whole days (and in the beginning, whole months) of craving him from the very bottom of my sternum, I could not escape or pretend away or second-guess the titanium truth that he was gone from my life, though he just hadn't departed it yet. There was not the slightest possibility of a second chance. My bad behavior, all of my mistakes, everything I failed to say or he failed to answer was now sealed into the immovable past, opaque to later examinations, I was afraid.

It is an awful, just sickening feeling, I discovered, to live with somebody, to exist in the midst of sharing a life, only to realize it is utterly doomed. It was botulism of the soul. I'd had such ambition for building a life together, because I wanted that strength of character and security. But I had overlooked the most important thing: he wasn't right for me. I wasn't right for him. Merely wanting us to be right and good together wasn't enough. It was only enough to sputter through about a decade.

I lost the ability to sleep. It was like I forgot how. I lay there and simply waited for something that did not arrive. There was no tiredness in me, but there was an exhaustion that ran much deeper, roiling like a river.

I also lost the ability to care, even slightly, about anything. I wasn't suicidal, because deep inside the suicidal impulse, when you cut it open and look at the pit, you see faith, which is like hope without the question mark.

People cannot get what they need in this life, so they decide to give themselves the relief of an end. They care enough to generate a desire and then take the action required to fulfill this desire. It isn't logical; there is no relief with suicide. But they believe there is. They know there is. That's faith. And I lost that. So I wasn't in any danger of swallowing the correct pills or cutting myself and bleeding it all away.

I was without that tiny hook you feel each day, the one that makes you change the sheets or go to work or feed the baby or eat. So while I wasn't even remotely suicidal, I was now the easiest of targets. My firewall was off. Had I found a tumor on my chest, noticing that it was there is all the action I would have taken.

———

We never laughed, Dennis and I. It was just not something we'd ever settled into with each other, an easy, over-nothing-really kind of laughter. That simply never came.

Years before we moved to Massachusetts, a magazine photographed us at Dennis's apartment on the Upper West Side. They'd placed us side by side on the sofa, and the photographer had said, "Okay, big smiles!"

We obliged. I think we both felt somewhat stiff and awkward.

She said, "Okay, now let's see some laughter." This proved more difficult. As a countermeasure to our grim attempts at joy, she encouraged us to go bigger. "Throw your head back!"

The pictures that ran in the magazine were atrocious. Manufactured happiness, complete with glaringly obvious flaws from the manufacturing process. But instead of hating these pictures, I now understand I should have learned from them. The awful photos were in fact my teacher. I just chose to skip the lecture.

Dennis was not a funny man. He was serious, intent on locating flaws, errors, and miscalculations. And I was not funny when I was around him, which was continuously. So if I ever had been funny, I wasn't anymore. I felt geriatric, like we should go ahead and move into his dad's nursing home.

One evening, I could no longer stand the awful, good-mannered silence that had swallowed us. I asked him, "When did you realize you had fallen out of love with me? Do you remember?"

There was silence, so I helped things along. "Was it a week ago? A month? Two months? Years?"

At first, he said nothing. He cleared his throat, and then

he coughed. By this point, I was no longer expecting an answer; that door had already closed. I would go upstairs and get something carbonated to drink.

Then in a voice so soft and low he could almost deny its existence, he said, "About a year. Less than a year."

Even as I asked the question, I half believed in the possibility that he would reply, "I didn't fall out of love with you." This would have sent me back to reevaluate everything. But because he had an answer, this made the thing I knew already to be true into an actual true thing that existed outside my own head.

He then said he had never felt so unattractive in his life, that he never expected to be in such a relationship, and that if he was ten years younger, he might not want to stay in it. He said he was too old and tired to start again, so we should just make it work.

How Cary Grant of him, I thought, masking my hurt and surprise with sarcasm.

I was making the bed as we had this conversation. I told him, "I don't want to be with somebody because he has a strong sense of duty." I imagined that if Dennis knew he had financial security, he wouldn't have stayed with me.

Earlier that summer, I started wearing a tiny stud earring in the hole I've had in my left ear since I was a teenager. He presented me with a box for my birthday, saying, "I noticed you started wearing an earring, so." I opened the box, and there was a pair of blue topaz earrings, surrounded by diamond chips. A ballerina setting, I believe it's called. Like Princess Diana's engagement ring. I laughed at first, because I thought it was a joke.

Dennis was deeply hurt by my reaction, and I realized instantly he'd been serious. He'd actually expected me to wear the earring, which would have looked lovely on somebody who wore glittery sweaters at Christmas and low beige heels. Inside each gift he gave me, I always sensed a little hidden package of anger. He was resentful as hell that he was the only one out there in the yard with the leaf blower. He did not approve of a man wearing an earring. But to be supportive, he'd bought me earrings for my birthday. But they were stained with his own judgment on the subject. So while they were hilarious when I thought he was kidding, they became insufferable when I realized he was not.

Perhaps the feeling overriding everything else was just the sad realization that this gift was physical evidence—proof—that he didn't know the very first thing about who I actually was. As though he'd been too busy studying me for flaws and incompatibilities to actually get to know me.

As the nights ground on and I worked more, I started feeling even more depressed. Emotional gravity set in. A swell of "This can't be real" overtook me, and it seemed like the most horrible thing ever. I realized just how out of love with me he was. He didn't even *like* me. But I generated cash. I was alone with him in this terrible dream house. It was exactly like Maggie and Brick. "I'm not living with you. We occupy the same cage, that's all."

I couldn't be with somebody who couldn't stand me. That's crazy.

If I vacuumed the downstairs? Dennis would hear the

vacuum and come downstairs and vacuum over again. If I dusted, he dusted the areas I just dusted. So I just stopped attempting any of these domestic chores because, frankly, I didn't give a fuck if the house was dusty. We live in a universe filled with dust. To fight it is to fight against the flow of time itself.

If I moved something in the medicine cabinet because I used it every morning, when I next opened the cabinet, it was back where he'd placed it, behind the taller things that are mostly never used. This is how it was: the warfare of our relationship played out wordlessly through a medicine cabinet.

He said he wanted to work on us. But his eyes said, "It's too late." And they had great shards of rage in them.

The only reason we were together now was because it's a lot of work to break up. I saw him at eight in the morning when he walked the dogs. Then again at midnight when he said good night to them.

So there I was in bed at two in the morning. But instead of sleeping, I had my laptop on my thighs, and I was squinting at the screen and typing a quick piece of code—chmod + x ~/.scripts/culturealarm—so that my computer's arcane Linux operating system would wake me each morning with the top video on YouTube.

As I strained to double-check the tiny white monospace characters of my command in the terminal emulator window, I saw something out of the corner of my eye. It was like a great shadow had crossed a wall or lightning had flashed in the distant corner of the room. I could not identify what I had seen, but inexplicably, I felt the rush of blind yet unmistakable lust.

Lust was disconcerting; it was not a part of my feeling world but rather something I vaguely remembered from my twenties with George, a sensation from the last century reserved for doomed bankers.

I clicked the Linux nonsense out of the way and spotted the coy slideshow widget on the desktop. While I was focused on my exacting, geeky task, my right eyeball had been busy scoping out the photographs without my knowledge. The slideshow widget fed from a file of photos somebody recently sent. They were not my pictures, but I knew most of the people in them.

"Who the fuck is that?" I said, but only in my mind because the person I vowed to spend the rest of my life with was asleep on the other side of the mattress. I checked on him to make sure he hadn't heard the racket going on inside my body, but he was asleep. So I looked back at the widget and leaned forward, nearly pressing my oily nose to the screen in order to scrutinize the picture.

It vanished, replaced by a photo of a collie.

I actually flinched, as though I had lost my footing and stepped off the edge of a backyard deck, my body anticipating the crack of the hard earth. A quick jab at the picture frame thing with my pointer brought back the previous image.

I stared. My throat was dry. A prickle of sweat stung my head.

It had actually only taken a mere thousandth of a second for me to recognize the person in the photograph. Hardly surprising; there are more neurons in the brain than there are stars in the known universe, and recognizing somebody one has known for ten years and speaks to every day—either in person or in e-mail—is not such a drain on one's neural resources. Not like, say, being the first to decipher hieroglyphics.

But tucked inside that fraction of a moment, it seemed to take an eternity for those familiar features to at last resolve into. . . . what? And before they did, before I was able to name the person, I was able to form the feeling: "I would die for him."

First, I felt love. Second, it was like a fist had been jammed into my crotch and pressed against my balls, an ache. I felt ownership, primal, just a mouth going, "Mine, mine, mine." And there at last it was: absolute recognition. And: Are you fucking kidding me? Not again. This. Is. Not. Possible.

This is my agent.

Under his suit, out of his office, Christopher reclined in a hammock and looked into the camera, lens flare, his hair swept away from his face, a face more beautiful than I'd allowed myself to realize in years. I'd spent so much time dissecting his flaws, a process that always made him laugh.

I despised whoever took that photograph, but I could not look away.

It felt as if I had just walked in on my boss in the bathroom stall at the office and he was whacking off, a Barbie Thumbelina in his free hand and a poppers-soaked dust mask covering his mouth. Except my dick was hard, much harder than it'd been in over a decade. So in this case, I was also my boss, and I had walked in on myself.

This is the first symptom of a brain disorder, I thought earnestly.

I wondered if I could make the picture larger.

Following the initial electrical discharge of distaste, my galaxy of neurons was once again able to provide me with a net of something akin to reason.

"Well, it's a very flattering picture. And I don't believe I've seen that hairstyle before. It's also very late, and I'm wiped out. So this whole thing, actually, it's funny!"

Then another voice, also inside my own head, spoke up. "It never went away, did it?"

The day I first saw Christopher, when he turned off Hudson Street and came walking toward me on Gansevoort Street, I could see the V of flesh at the top of his shirt from a half block away, and something about his hair made me want to grip his head and run my fingers through it.

Over the years, I'd noticed that everybody who greeted him hugged and kissed him hello and good-bye except me. Why was that, exactly? When it came time for us to say good-bye, there was a stiff handshake, possibly a snide remark from me, but absolutely no hint from him that we should hug and kiss, too.

The voice in my head said, "Please. This is something new?"

This was very much like going through rehab for alcoholism or drug abuse: your substance of choice was ruined forever. Oh, you could drink again, and you could snort away your 401(k)—or what was left of it—but not for one instant would you fall down the lovely rabbit hole of complete oblivion. Because now, you know. And knowledge spoils everything. Unfortunately, one can never un-know something.

It was like that with Christopher. Before the picture: *you pulled it off, told yourself he was off-limits and turned your mind away from him.* After the picture: *you're in love; you're in lust; you're in trouble.*

Dennis was still asleep, and the room was silent. I stared over the laptop screen into the dark, and my mind throbbed, *Wow, wow, wow, wow, fuck.*

The phrase "in the pit of your stomach," I realized, is fully accurate. For there did seem to be a central pit located inside me. The pit contained facts cloaked in darkness. Gleaming things in hiding. Sparkly threads of gold, hairs on a wrist. Now, a hammock with a nearly naked man enveloped in it. It was my own junk drawer, filled with the tangled truth.

I actually suggested to myself, *Now that I have acknowledged it, it will go away.*

As I discovered over the following days, that was not precisely what occurred. Rather, I found myself even more distracted.

"Where is that wetsuit picture, the one from Saint Lucia?" I wondered, scrolling wildly through my image files.

My photo file contained several images of Christopher from some past life, most taken at an unknown beach at an unknown time. This activity inspired within me a feeling akin to swallowing one's own child's pain medication: "God, I am a sick and horrible person. But where the fuck is that pill?"

Meanwhile, it was business as usual. "Hey, what's up? Did I tell you that my life with Dennis is totally falling apart because I feel like he hates me and I'm not in love with him, which means I signed away half the rights to all my books to somebody who would totally benefit if I had fatal illness?"

Because nothing had changed on Christopher's end, I felt extra insane. Something had shifted inside of me, and normally, he was the very person I would have told. But I couldn't tell him, I'd become fixated on pictures of him.

"Hey, check this out. I haven't told anybody else, but I'm growing a tail. Just lemme get this belt undone, and I'll show you. Soon it'll be too big to keep tucked inside. I'm gonna have to see somebody about it."

I had stuffed him and my feelings for him as far down as I could, and for a few years there, I even convinced myself that it worked. Living in Massachusetts had put physical distance between us; I couldn't just drop into the office, and our homes were no longer a mere seven blocks apart. I still saved my cruelest and funniest lines for him, but they were frequently directed *at* him, a pathetic attempt to minimize him in my brain and in my heart. He brought out the worst in me but in the best possible way. What he brought out in me was the truth, and it wasn't always beautiful or handsome.

I'd watched him cycle through a couple of relationships while I myself met somebody and decided to fall in love and create a stable life for myself.

Yeah, I did that. I *decided* to fall in love. God sees that remark, and he circles it with his big red felt pen, chuckling.

My relationship with Dennis had closed the door and locked it on *my agent*. He was single again, had been for a few years, and according to him, would be for the rest of his life. Professing to be tired and old, he claimed that his large circle of friends and his ability to find uncomplicated sex would be enough. He didn't have the energy, he said, "to tell my entire fucking story to someone. It's also why I don't get back into therapy. My crust is now armorlike."

If I felt a flicker of jealousy at the time, it was too deeply buried for me to acknowledge it. I made a joke about a team in hazmat outfits having to come in and burn the sheets after he and some other infected old man covered them with their sex disease, and of course he laughed, though of course it just wasn't funny.

It took something terrible to punch the truth out of my stomach and allow me to realize an attraction remained.

I was in a hotel room in LA with Dennis when Christopher called to tell me he had cancer. He couched the news with this: luckily, it was Hodgkin's—"the good cancer"—and really there was nothing to worry about. Our mutual friend David had Hodgkin's when he was in his twenties, and Christopher said David told him, "Aside from thyroid cancer, which is treated with a milk shake, this is the most desirable one available."

I felt a wishbone lodged in my throat when I tried to swallow and breathe. I also made a wisecrack, something to lance the moment, drain it of its significance, reassure him of the normalcy of life.

When I hung up the phone, it was shocking to feel my body begin to convulse without permission, to heave for air as I cried. When was the last time I'd cried? Maybe 1982? I was astounded that such a magnitude of physical motion was even possible against my will or knowledge. It was like sneezing for twenty minutes, plus a broken heart.

I cried past the point of grief, so far past it that I was able to sit on my hotel mattress and say, "Okay, this is idiotic now. I never cry. And I can't stop. It's so Julianne Moore. Is something broken?" When I walked into the bathroom and looked at myself in the mirror, I laughed out loud at what a wreck I was, all puffy and leaky. Which brought on another wave.

It's like he knew about the hammock picture, that he had access to the contents of my brain as I saw it, and now he was making himself even further off-limits with a new death-threatening illness. He was stoic, facing six months of chemotherapy alone. Oh, surrounded by dozens of friends and a nearly 150-pound dog, to be sure. But alone. And this felt wrong, like a clerical error.

I swooned. I wondered if all those feelings could be fatal. If my brain could be overwhelmed, too much blood sent to the surface convolutions of the brain itself, causing a hemorrhage. It seemed dangerous to think of them.

My doggedly, Catholically loyal partner was right there in the room with me through it all. He even handed me tissues and told me to press an icy washcloth to my eyes to reduce the swelling. Horribly, I did think, *Why couldn't it be him?* When I glanced over at Dennis, I was certain he could read my thoughts, so I turned away.

When I next saw Christopher, he was bald and old and impossibly fat.

"They're giving me steroids to keep my energy up, which also increases my appetite, and then I gain weight," he explained. "So I lost my hair and got fat. I'm getting Uncle Fester chemo."

It shocked me so much that during lunch I bit the inside of my cheek four times, having misplaced the exact location of my own teeth. He was genuinely upbeat and charming while I was genuinely terrified and struck by awe. He physically revolted me, and I realized, *I love him so permanently.*

The next time I saw him was three months after his treatment ended. Dennis and I were joining him for dinner.

We were slightly late. Also, we stank like acrid sweat, because we'd been wordlessly arguing in the car on the way into the city from Massachusetts.

Christopher was already seated at the table, and in all the years I had known the man, he had never looked so fine. Vigorous and healthy, free not only from cancer but from everything else that clings to a person and diminishes them.

Years were missing from his face.

Radiance, when actually encountered in a person, causes you to blink.

He fought cancer, and look who won.

I could not take my watery eyes off him. I could feel Dennis's quizzical stare, but I could not look away from the man before me, my agent, my best friend. He was heroic. And standing there before him, pulling my chair out, finally, to be seated, I surprised both of us by reaching out and gripping the back of his chair. My knuckles dragged against the back of his neck, briefly.

Burning-faced, I sat. Lopsided, blundering, I experienced a seasickness of full-force physical attraction.

I ordered the steak.

When his leg knocked against mine under the table by accident, I came very close to spitting chewed meat onto the tablecloth. I wanted to literally run from the restaurant, fleeing on foot.

His spirits were great. He was so funny. If only Dennis hadn't been there souring the evening with his endless series of tedious questions. "Were the nurses nice? I've heard that's a pleasant hospital. Is it true? Was the chemo difficult to work into your schedule?" He reeked of smallness. And I loathed myself most for reaching the point where all I could see were his flaws, whether real or conjured.

I was possessed with the most curious sense of urgency. Anyone who wasn't Christopher was wasting my time. Dinner was over in mere minutes, it seemed to me, which only heightened the sense that I had to *do* something, *say* something, take immediate action.

The drive back to Amherst seemed four times as long as the trip out. But "home" offered many distractions: a routine, work, my dogs, e-mailing my friends, my slot, my rut, my rot.

A week passed.

The dinner, the accidental knocking of his leg under the table, the way my senses became all mixed up and the way the light in the restaurant had made his hair sweet-smelling, how when he spoke, it felt as though I was about to board an ocean liner.

I was presented with a gift. It arrived in the form of certainty. Certain things, true things, facts that are made of foot-thick steel and anchored miles deep into the earth, are comforting because they provide a fulcrum around which you work or plan or live or figure things out. This is what I knew, my certainty: the thing I felt for the man who was my agent had established roots. It existed; it would continue to exist. It had been there when I first met him, and instead of evaporating, it had penetrated.

Instead of causing me to panic, oddly, this knowledge generated a tiny metallic click deep and low in my brain. *Unlocked.* It set me free. This great freedom came as an understanding that I need not move a muscle. Not all dots should be connected. I was free to love one person but live with someone else. People did that all the time. It was sad, yes. But kind of beautiful, too, right?

I closed my eyes and rested my head against the back of my chair. The steady beating of my heart inside my chest sounded like "Nope-*nope*, nope-*nope*, nope-*nope*."

I called bullshit on myself.

There was freedom, and then there was everything else. Freedom didn't come in degrees. It was an all-or-nothing proposition.

I wanted it all.

Several weeks after dinner with Christopher, Dennis seemed particularly unhappy. It wasn't that he was grumpier than usual; he was even more distant. And when we did run into each other in the kitchen or on the stairs, he was exceedingly polite. I read in his smile a distinct warning. So instead of confronting him, I e-mailed him even though there was just one floor between us. I told him I knew something was wrong, could he just maybe tell me about it in a letter?

It turned out, he could. He provided me with a list several pages long of all the things he loathed about me.

He followed this up with the suggestion that we see a couples' therapist.

The list was like a blueprint of who I was as a person, and it included my choice of beverage, my nervous tics, and scores of other personal details, many beyond my control. The list was shocking to read: so many years of pent-up resentments unspooling before me on my laptop screen, a careful itemization crafted by the son of an accountant. All along, there had been "something the matter," and all these years, he'd said there was not. The list was proof of his spectacular betrayal. The list was also the single thing I must have required to clarify my own position in my own mind, because now, it was over. At the end of the list, he made a lame apology about how he knew it was bad to keep all this stuff inside and that this was a beginning for him; he was finally talking about it.

But this was no beginning for me. This was the end.

Through a reply e-mail, I agreed to see a therapist, but I needed to be clear about why. I told him to come downstairs and help me make the bed. That's when I told him.

"This isn't to work things out between us, to save the relationship, because there is no relationship to save," I told him. "You don't want me. I make you miserable. I won't ever want to go snowshoeing in Aspen, I will never have enough of what you want, and I will always have too much of everything you hate. We aren't good for each other. And I will see a therapist with you so that you understand and believe that it's over."

I didn't know how Dennis felt about that. Did he want us to be over? Or did he want to stay together? He just nodded and made hospital corners with the sheet.

I believed he loved the life we built, the oil-bronze-finished door pulls, the closets filled with linens, the cars. I definitely felt our life would be perfect for him if only I wasn't in it. Our primary problem had been communication. While he would admit to having "hatred issues" with me, he wouldn't go into the specifics. "Hatred issues" was enough for me. I felt like if you have hatred issues for the person you're with, especially if you can catalog them, maybe it's time to reevaluate your situation.

Were the things he hated about me the same things I hated about myself? Or by sharing, would he give me all new things to despise? It was looking like I might never know. I wanted to end our relationship neatly, with a bow if possible. Something that resembled resolution, a truce. Perhaps therapy would be this pretty bow, even though my history with therapy had been more lumpy packages with terrible surprises inside.

At the recommendation of a physician I barely knew, we ended up in the office of a Manhattan therapist plucked from a different era. She had 1970s Joyce Carol Oates hair, a full regalia of filigree sterling silver and malachite jewelry. Even in repose, she leaned forward slightly, as if reaching for a teak-handled skewer in a fondue pot.

There may have been spider plants, and they may have been hanging. I cannot be sure, because it was difficult to lift my eyes off the Pottery Barn lamp from back in the days when Pottery Barn was a fruit crate of a store that sold chipped earthenware to slightly unwashed people who smelled like frankincense. The therapist's office itself had the aroma of beeswax and wet cork. But mostly, it smelled like sickness of the mind.

Dennis sat to my left on the sofa, I was in a shabby chair (the "chic" part had long worn away), and the therapist sat in the command chair across from us.

I felt no hatred for Dennis. Looking at him seated on the couch with his hands curled into tender fists on his lap, I felt the sickness of heartbreak, which was compounded by the feeling that I had skipped ahead and read the last chapter. I already knew how this story turned out.

This was because I had insider information: a crime in Wall Street circles; one that can land you in prison for twenty years and slap you with a $25 million fine. It was, however, a particularly valuable piece of interpersonal intel, and I was ready to deploy it: there was zero hope for us. Dennis was still of the opinion that there was something to work out; a compromise to be made and in which we could live. But this was not the case. There would be no compromise, because I was done with that.

What I saw with such clarity that day was that life is, indeed, not simply black and white but rather the gray that results from blending the two together. The *black* I felt at Dennis's bewilderment at how swiftly the world came crumbling down around him, all because of some silly list he'd been keeping about my flaws, which I saw as proof that he'd been lying to me for years.

The *white* was the cotton sheet blowing in the sun that I felt when I fantasized about Christopher, propped up against a mound of pillows somewhere and me tracing just one finger around and around each shirt button, sliding my finger through the opened vents between them. Then, trailing my finger down the side of his chest, bump, bump, bumping over the ribs until I reached his belt buckle, where my finger would pause, like Thelma and Louise on the edge of the cliff.

Dennis began to outline in the briefest, most orderly fashion the despair he'd felt with me for years. I remembered his personal ad, how well written and amusing it was, hinting at a playfulness, which, if it ever truly existed, had been flattened into a grinding daily sorrow. And because I felt betrayed, having asked him every day, "Are you sure you're happy?" and he'd replied to my face, "Yes, I'm sure," I didn't feel like quite as much of a scumbag as I might have for letting my eyes drift away from his downturned mouth as he spoke and fixing my gaze on the atrocious broken-tile mosaic hanging on the wall while I visualized that finger of mine still parked on the edge of my agent's belt buckle, my gaze on the swell in the crotch of his pants, my eyes drilling into strained fabric over the zipper.

The therapist's strident voice startled me out of my soft-core daydream.

She said there was reason to be optimistic, that many couples could save their marriages through therapy. Something in her manner made me expect that at any moment she would pull a small deerskin drum out from under her chair and say, "Deep breathing and rhythmic drumming are powerful tools for mending a marriage. So is sage."

I felt there could be no ambiguity. I barked, "I just need to say, we're not here to repair this. He needs to understand that it has ended. He needs to be perfectly clear that reuniting is not within the realm of possibility and that—"

She cut me off and motioned with the palms of her hands as if to push me back. "That's enough," she said. "One step at a time. This is a process. That's an awful lot to digest all at once."

Then she suggested ten sessions. Five plus five, a neat fair number, just right for the fifty-fifty partnership between two people.

I said, "I don't believe it will be helpful to give him false hope." I saw no reason this couldn't be resolved within the next twenty minutes.

Her features tightened, and her mouth became a straight little line. She did not care for my bossy, let's-cut-to-the-chase-here outbursts one bit. Her eyes said, "Shut the fuck up, asshole."

"And I don't believe," she said, "that we should enter into therapy knowing in advance how we expect it to turn out."

I smiled back at her and replied, "I'm sorry. I know you want me to take a time-out, and I apologize, but I'm going to say something else." And I told her I was worried about Dennis and his ability to terminate his denial. I explained that he had already been in therapy for nearly fifteen years.

Though I didn't add, "And you can see for yourself how useless it was."

I spoke pointedly, I felt, but not disrespectfully. Like one doctor to another, except that I'm the opposite of a doctor and way more like a patient who tied the doctor up, locked him in the nurses' lounge, and is now at a shopping mall wearing his doctor's clothes.

But I was truly worried. Once Dennis realized I was gone, it would hit him hard, and he would need somebody with Joyce Carol Oates hair to steady him. Either that or he would be just manic with relief and giddy with possibility, in which case he would also need her, if only to affirm for him, "But of course it's okay for you to celebrate without feeling guilty. I saw him. He was a monster!"

She turned to Dennis and asked him, "How long have you been unhappy in this relationship with Augusten?"

Dennis shot me a bashful, sideways glance and then looked back at her before looking down at his own lap. Sullenly, he replied, "A few years. I mean, the first two were really good, but after that . . ." He let the thought to just drop right there, baby-on-the-church-steps style.

My hands gripped the well-worn arms of the Naugahyde armchair. "You were happy for two years, that's it?" I wanted to shout, "But that leaves eight! That means you lied to me on a daily basis for eight motherfucking years!" (Later, I did the math: 2,920 lies.)

Even though I didn't say this or anything else, the therapist had her eye on me and her hand was already outstretched, like she was petsitting a friend's ungainly Saint Bernard and warning it away from the coffee table. She again suggested we agree to ten more sessions. I thought, *She's only interested in slamming shut my blustering window so that all the cash doesn't blow out it.* At least if she'd said, "How about this: ten more sessions and I'll throw in a set of four earthenware daisy mugs and a toaster oven," at least I could have respected her motives.

One of the items on Dennis's "One Million Things I Hate About Augusten" list was that he thought I had a forceful personality. Well, that was better than having a simpering, lying, weak personality like he did. I wanted to take that list of his and shove it down his throat.

The fact that Joyce Carol Oates was using the identical hand signals with me that a traffic cop would use to stop a cement truck from barreling through an intersection populated with children from a church group did appear to legitimize his complaint, if only slightly. She turned to Dennis, and when he spoke, he did so in a soft, hesitant voice. Carefully, he described me as a "bully," and I thought, *Yeah, but only in comparison to someone who sucks in his lips and bites them so he won't say something terrible and coughs instead of having meaningful conversation.*

I didn't actually roll my eyes, but I did think, *I may have had the louder voice, but he had the sharper words.* Still, I had to admit it was a good strategic move on his part. He'd totally won her over to his side with that one, because Dr. Crochet Sweater Vest would like nothing more than to stab me in the eye with her "A Woman Without a Man Is Like a Fish Without a Bicycle" button.

As the session drew to a close, it was agreed that we would return, Dennis first, for a one-on-one.

Outside on the sidewalk, I said, "Well, at least she got to see me be a bully."

And though it was small and sad, Dennis laughed for the first time in what seemed like years.

I knew he did not understand why I stuffed a bouquet of dynamite into the crevice that had opened between us, lit it, and watched it blow us completely apart. But I did contain hope within my chest that someday, he would understand. Perhaps we'd been not in a relationship together, after all, so much as crouching together in the same hiding space, a true limited liability partnership.

Maybe for a time, the fact that both of us wanted it to work made up for the fact that it really never did. With the relationship over, I wasn't sure if we would even be friends. It didn't seem likely we'd even be left with that.

Two years before, we'd bought a studio apartment in downtown New York City. The plan had been to fix it up like a hotel room so we could return to Manhattan whenever we wanted and not be trapped in the country, which is exactly what we were. But we'd never furnished it. In fact, it contained only a floor lamp and an air mattress, also on the floor. I would be staying in the New York apartment, and he would return to the house in Amherst.

It was awkward standing there on the sidewalk outside the therapist's brownstone, because we weren't accustomed to going in opposite directions. We nodded solemnly and agreed we'd be in touch before the next session. He asked me to gather any mail that came and send it on to him. He said if there was mail for me back in Amherst, he'd bring it with him to the next therapy appointment. Moments before, we had been confronting our most devastating, life-changing feelings and shredding the fabric of our decade together, and now he was scheduling mail delivery.

As I walked away, I felt a kind of speedy sadness, raw-nerved. My eyes felt like they must be ringed with red. At the same time, I felt an urgency in my chest, not like butterflies but rather more like crows were wrestling inside, beating their wings against my rib cage.

I was free.

And didn't this mean, wasn't it possible, I might have another chance? To find somebody I wouldn't have to change for, somebody who wasn't bothered so much by the many troublesome things about me or maybe even liked them?

When I had first started dating after meeting him and deeming him unacceptable, I believed I could find "somebody like Christopher," but that was ridiculous. I didn't want somebody *like* Christopher. He was the only one like him. That's the one I wanted. What if I just went ahead and told him how I felt? How I'd felt all along? So what if he laughed in my face and then fired me as his client and had me blacklisted from publishing? At least I could tell myself that I'd seen the thing I wanted, and I'd chased after it.

Dennis had hurt me. He'd lied to me for so many years, shoplifting time that belonged to me. But as I crossed Broadway, another thought came into my mind. Each time I asked Dennis, "Are you happy with me?" what if I was really asking this of myself?

What if I had been the one lying?

What if the only person I could blame was myself?

I passed one of those ubiquitous Irish pubs with neon clovers in the windows and signs for Pabst on tap. I knew that if I walked into that pub, it would be dank and cool and dark and that I could slide onto a well-polished bar stool and order a tumbler of vodka or maybe a gin and tonic. I also knew, after two or three of these, all blame would recede from me as surely as an ocean tide. Nothing would be my fault.

The catch was I could never leave the bar.

I walked past it. Sober for yet another fucked-up, mistake-drenched day. But there was one hell of a wind blowing against my back, and it almost made walking as easy as one of those sliding airport walkways. In that moment, it kind of felt like a present from the universe.

Several days later, the doctor who referred us to the '70s patchouli therapist called. He'd received a message from the therapist saying she was unwilling to see me and Dennis again. That seemed a little unprofessional. Shouldn't she have contacted me herself? Surely such a roundabout message was in violation of something, and certainly she should be punished.

On the other hand, I appreciated the swift efficiency of her act. The brutal reality of it. Like a Joyce Carol Oates novel.

It reminded me of when I first started to go bald. I went in for a haircut, and my hairdresser sat me down as usual, poised the shears over my head, and then reconsidered and put them down. He grabbed the clippers.

"Why no scissors all of a sudden?" I'd asked, genuinely curious.

He leveled a gaze at me in the mirror and then glanced down at what was left of my hair. He wasn't mean about it, but he shrugged and said, "Not really much point anymore, you know? Clippers for you from now on."

Looking at myself fresh through his eyes, I suddenly saw that what was actually on top of my head was not so much hair as the fuzzy remains of my own denial. *Motherfucker.*

In my empty studio apartment, I thought about Dennis. I imagined he must have been so lonely to occupy the same house, the same life with somebody who couldn't have sex with him and who didn't even see how brutally unhappy he was.

He said to me once that he felt responsible for staying. He said that so many bad things had happened to me, he could not bear to be another one of them. So he stayed. I was the one who left. I was the one who tore apart our lives. But I did it for him as much as for me. I did it because I could, and he could not.

Molly told me, "Divorce is like a Polaroid picture. What truly happened will develop over time, and you will see."

She was right about that.

To admit early on that we seemed incompatible, unable to communicate freely and easily and honestly, would have felt like an act of such savage destruction. We were making plans for our fine, good life together, and they would to have been thrown away. Which is exactly what happened, only much later and leaving behind a much larger debris field.

I know now: what *is* is all that matters. Not the thing

you know is meant to be, not what could be, not what should be, not what ought to be, not what once was.

Only the *is*.

I bought furniture for the apartment, and after ten years of living with somebody, I was on my own again. I missed my dogs. Dennis offered to drive into the city with them and let me have them on weekends, but I found myself worrying about him being alone in the house we built, the one we used to share, if he didn't have the dogs, without something to worry about and take care of.

My instincts told me that no matter how hard it was for me to be without them, no matter how closely the physical ache I felt without them resembled impending heart failure, it would be worse for Dennis. After all, wasn't I the expert at losing things?

When the dogs were with me, I was grateful. I didn't have an actual job, so I could spend all of every prized day on the bed with them both.

I shopped online for vintage jewelry to comfort myself. My grandmother had been one of those Southern ladies who dripped with jade bangles, diamond rings, emerald necklaces, and earrings of beaded rubies. Since I was a little boy, I have loved all things shiny and sparkly. Now, because I had no control or judgment or real-world knowledge, I was siphoning my 401(k) to buy them.

I scrolled through Web site images of jade rings. I climbed up off the bed to get treats for the sleeping bulldogs.

Add to cart, add to cart.

III

I sent Christopher an e-mail telling him how I felt. An e-mail seemed better than a phone call or a meeting in person, because he was accustomed to me dumping my words all over him. Plus, it was how I was most comfortable, and I couldn't screw it up.

Christopher,

Two things. First, did you ever hear back from the sub-rights agent about a sale for India?

The other thing is slightly out of the blue. I love you, is the thing. And I mean *love* love, not *love you, bro.* I mean, I am in love with you, and it's an eye-color kind of love, unchangeable and bright. I know this must be somewhat shocking (appalling?) to you, because you've never given any indication that you felt anything but professional agent friendliness for me, but I have felt much more for so long it's possibly caused me brain damage. Also, I am certain you love me, too. Or at least mostly certain. Or at least I hope.

What I want is for you to cab downtown right now so we can quickly go over to city hall and get married. I don't want us to be agent and client for one more moment. I want us to be together, permanently. I also need to know certain things about you. For example, I can't even remember your birthday. Also, I've never seen pictures of your childhood house, or better yet, heard you describe it. I don't even know if you had stuffed animals as a kid.

I want to know everything. Shoe size, dental history, allergies, favorite color, special abilities or skills, gluten tolerance level. I require complete knowledge and 100 percent access to all of you. I am like the fat girl at a buffet with three plates balanced on her arm like a waitress. "That bitch, did you see her? She just took all the Bac-Os." My greed and hunger with respect to you are without limit.

You should know, I tried for many years not to be in love with you, but I failed. And I really did try very hard. But it was not possible, and it never has been, because I have actually loved you from very early in our relationship. Possibly as early as our first meeting.

A small part of me is aware that this might be somewhat blindsiding for you. I also know it's gross for the famous author to fall in love with his literary agent, but on the flip side? At least we're not twenty-four. That's what saves us from being entirely repulsive as a couple. In fact, it's almost romantic, isn't it? Like Charles and Camilla.

And no, I'm not drunk.

He wrote me back pretty quickly. "Well, that certainly qualifies as your most shocking piece of writing in my learned opinion. But as fascinating and flattering and strangely hallucinatory as I found it, it can't possibly be true. I am a crusty old sack of disease with holes blown through it, like a horror movie character that can't be killed. Which makes you, sir, crazy. So snap out of it," he concluded. "This is just a phase."

His reply was very much the words of a literary agent caught off guard, defusing his unstable writer.

I replied, "Will you at least consider trying to see me as more than just a client?"

He wrote back, "I have AIDS and cancer, and you're a Purell addict."

"Plus short," I reminded him. "Everything you said so far plus short." I also told him that I'd never been as sure about anything else. I said, "I'd already lost one boyfriend to AIDS when I was in my twenties, and I decided never again. So when I met you, you were off-limits. I decided I couldn't love you. The problem was, I did. And ten years later, here we are. All those reasons I had for it being impossible between us, they're nothing. I'm not just in love with you. I'm insanely in love with you."

He called me then so that I could hear his laughter in my actual fat ear and not read *LOL* on screen.

I asked him if he would meet me in Hell's Kitchen for burgers.

"Be there in twenty," he said.

We went to a sports bar near Worldwide Plaza on Forty-Ninth. As soon as we were seated, I knew. I could see it in his eyes as surely as their color: he loved me, too. He did. There was disbelief there, too, but there was no doubt.

"This is crazy," he said.

I reached under the table while the Yankees got clobbered, and I traced my finger along his calf.

"You know what else it is?" I asked him, feeling the hairs through his pants. "It's happening."

Christopher had never thought of me in romantic terms. He said this and even used that word *terms*, ever the commission-sucking agent. Whereas I had been thinking of him lustfully for an alarmingly long time. Yet, there over burgers, there was a transformation. His perspective did shift, and he was quite able to see me as more than just a client, partly because I was groping him under the table and partly because we were by now the best of friends, able to laugh at the absurdity of the situation.

Near the end of the meal, I went to the bathroom to take a leak. I was shocked when I looked in the mirror and saw that a spot on the front of my pants was already wet, as though I'd pissed a little in them.

Maybe this was an actual nervous breakdown, I thought.

When I returned to the table, his face was flushed. He looked at the crotch of my jeans, and he knew, exactly. When he stood up, I could see he was hard. We were way too old and worn out for this shit, but there it was, right in front of us.

Dennis, meanwhile, still did not understand what had happened with our relationship. He sent an e-mail referring to our "trial separation."

I wrote back quickly. "This is not a separation." (I refused to include "trial," because it added a layer of hope and took a step away from truth.) "This is *the end*," I told him decisively. Yet he still e-mailed about my "coming home" despite my already feeling Massachusetts was another life, as remote as another planet.

Another sensitive area was Christopher's friendship with Dennis. Since they were not the ones who had lived together and grown to loathe one another, they had a good time when they went out. Christopher is bighearted, and he genuinely liked Dennis. It was also tough, because Dennis needed a confidant, and he knew that Christopher knew my crazy better than anyone.

Since I hadn't successfully convinced Dennis that we were broken up, Christopher and I felt weird about actually having sex. It was unlike either of us to show such moral fiber, but I didn't want infidelity heaped on top of any other accusations. What was it going to take to make him see?

The following week, *The New York Times* published an article about my newly decorated and highly eccentric apartment; Dennis was referred to as my "former partner" in one of the opening paragraphs. It was hard to ignore the message after that.

Ten or perhaps twelve minutes later, Christopher and I stood wearing jeans but no shirts in the tiny hallway of my studio apartment. As we moved in toward one another, I stopped and said, "What if one of us barfs?"

He said, "That's when we'll know this wild experiment has gone horribly wrong. But if it happens, I hope it's you."

Then it was like, "Oh, so *this* is sex." This is what all those therapists meant when they talked about how sex was a connection to another person. I'd never before experienced that. I'd never felt sex travel through my arms before. I'd never felt sex spread above the waist. I'd never come three times a day with such regularity. Near the end of—and for a while after—every orgasm, Christopher laughed. This made me crack up at the spectacle.

We destroyed the sheets. It was disgusting and awesome in equal measure. I stopped cleaning. I didn't care anymore about dust and grossness. I just wanted to be in bed with my agent and fuck all day. The one thing I hadn't expected was that he'd look so completely hot out of his clothes: he was naturally muscular, like a gymnast, and hairy, which was also good. Just well shaped all over. And his skin was so sensitive that I could raise goose bumps with just a single finger, hovering—not even touching—anywhere over his body. Crack was nothing compared to this high. Booze was less than zero.

I mashed my face up against his neck and pressed my body as tightly as I could against his. "I can't fucking get close enough to you," I said.

He pulled me even closer. He was *strong.*

"Would you marry me right this second if you could?" I asked.

"I would," he said.

"Are you sure?"

"Positive."

"Is sex with me better than with the other boyfriends?"

He laughed from his stomach, which was ribbed like a lobster's shell from laughing so much over the many years. "*Way.*"

"Are you still gonna take a fifteen percent commission?"

"No, of course not," he said, kissing me tenderly on the neck. Then he murmured forcefully into my jugular, "We'll start with twenty-five and see how it goes."

We couldn't tell anyone yet, that much was clear. At the very least, we had to continue our constant sex in order to figure out exactly what it was that we had before we could reveal it to anyone. We weren't going to tell my editor, Jen, or Christopher's agency colleagues or even any of our friends that this amazing thing had happened, if there were even the tiniest possibility that it could fizzle out three weeks later. That would have made for one of my most awkward "just kidding!" scenarios ever, and that's saying something. We both knew it was real and that the whole test-drive thing was basically over after our first official date. But we sure as hell weren't ready to tell Dennis, so it just seemed easier to not tell anyone.

The silver lining to being one another's dirty little secret was that it was hot. Sneaking around and holding on to wonderfully explosive information ratcheted up the already-boiling sexual tension and made it seem illicit and slightly unbelievable. We added to that illusion when we both went to a writers' conference in Boston and had wild sex in our hotel room between appointments.

That Sunday afternoon, we had a little under an hour before the train left for New York. Christopher and I are both speed eaters, so we decided to grab lunch at a pub across the street from Back Bay station. It had tables outside, and the grayish sky didn't look like it was actually going to pelt us with rain before our train left, so it seemed safe enough to eat outdoors.

Christopher loved the cold so much that he slept with the windows open in winter. He also loved plaid, so this so-chilly-but-not-freezing weather made him very happy, because he got to wear his blue plaid Windbreaker with the extra zippers.

We snarfed down our semi-good bacon cheeseburgers and fries, observing and inventing dramas being played out in the courtyard nearby. (The Asian woman holding the flower was being stood up by her blind date. Later, she'd have a Lean Cuisine dinner by herself and contemplate but not actually commit suicide.) The waitress cleared our plates, and Christopher signaled her for the check.

As he reached around for his wallet in his back pocket, he was smirking. He was prone to laughing for seemingly no reason, usually because he was thinking of a tweet he'd read or a video he'd seen—babies shooting off the backs of treadmills, brides tripping into swimming pools, that kind of thing delighted him. He was holding his nubby black electric eel-skin wallet, and my eyes were drawn to his fingers as he freed several ATM-fresh twenties. I glanced at his crotch and then at the horseshoe mustache that framed his smile. The sharp wind had popped the collar of his jacket, and it was flapping against his neck. He was eighties in the seventies, and he was eighties now; he was spectacular.

Watching him sitting there, his compactness was somehow more obvious than when he was standing. It made me gnash my teeth. He looked like . . . I couldn't quite say. I almost had it, but not quite. It was on the tip of my brain tongue.

I raised my phone and took his picture.

When I saw the shot, I instantly knew what it was. *Of course.*

I turned my phone around and showed it to him. I smiled. "Look," I said, "it's a chimp with a wallet and a big dick."

When Christopher laughed at indoor restaurants, he frequently got shushed. He laughed with gusto and volume, but that day, we were outside, and the rain had started, after all, so we were alone and nobody hushed him. For once.

"You are so awful!" he said when his roaring died down. He smirked again. "But at least I've got a wallet."

We were both laughing, and we couldn't stop, one wave crashing into another. The waiters watched us warily from inside the warm, dry restaurant. We were displaying much more joy than is customary in Boston, so we packed up our merriment and went to catch our train.

Once a month or so, Dennis would drive down to the city with the dogs. A few times, he left them with me for a couple of weeks, but he usually came in for a weekend to do New York things, so I got them in three-day bursts.

"Where does Dennis stay when he's in town?" Christopher asked.

"Here, in the apartment," I told him.

There was a short silence, and then he gave a sort of "no comment" snort.

"What?" I asked, knowing exactly.

"Nothing," he said. "It's just a little weird that when he comes into the city you sleep in the same bed."

He was right, of course. It was awful and awkward, and the only reason it was even possible was because it wouldn't be for much longer: reality was sinking in for Dennis. A few times, he'd already stayed with friends in Brooklyn instead. I saw this as progress.

Besides, who was Christopher to talk about exes sleeping over?

His apartment on the Upper West Side was like a New York City apartment in a movie. It had three bedrooms, two bathrooms, a kitchen with a swinging door, and a pantry. There was a piano in his bedroom, but if the door was closed, you couldn't hear him playing from the next room. That's how thick the old prewar walls were. The first thought I had when I walked in was, *If there's ever a nuclear blast in Manhattan, this is the place to be.*

It was rent stabilized, which is one notch down from the holy Manhattan grail of "rent controlled," and it belonged to his first boyfriend, Harvey, who died of AIDS.

The apartment was also occupied by Zeke, his brilliant and never-employed former boyfriend who bore a strong resemblance to George Clooney. Zeke was the boyfriend who moved in shortly after they began dating in the late

1990s, and after an amicable breakup, he simply never moved out.

Christopher was a hairy little madman who, in his own more adorable way, rivaled me maniacal act for maniacal act. He was also strictly an as-is guy, not a fixer-upper. An all-sales-final guy. He felt responsible for Zeke, like he would a mentally disabled brother, which I understood, except Zeke possessed an odd and appealing artistic genius. A mutual friend once said, "Zeke is not an idiot savant. He's a savant idiot," but regardless, his talents demonstrated far more mental ability than I myself possessed at that stage in my broken-down life. I sometimes felt Zeke needed to be kicked out of the nest. And then the tree needed to be sawed down so that Christopher and I could burn the wood for heat.

The funny thing is, when Christopher moved into his massive apartment twenty-eight years previously, he moved in with Harvey and Harvey's ex-boyfriend, who was still living there. So this was a learned behavior. This was why he didn't want to let it go: layers of history iced with mental illness.

It is also fair to say that twenty-eight years ago was the last time it was cleaned. It had no operational lighting in the kitchen (opening the refrigerator door would do) and no cold water in one of the bathrooms. It was perfectly insane, the residence of a deeply authentic eccentric, one with exceptional night vision.

If Christopher and I ever got married, Zeke would be part of the dowry. This seemed like it should be entirely unacceptable to me, except that it wasn't. I liked Zeke a lot. He was stark-raving mad in the best way. And I didn't care if there were no lights in the kitchen, because I happened to own several antique coal miner's lanterns, each in perfect working order.

History was important to Christopher.

He still had people from his youth that he saw with some frequency. He and four New York publishing friends had been meeting for breakfast every Thursday at the same diner since 1997. I mean, who has a Breakfast Club in real life?

He was not one to discard things; he gathered them.

I, on the other hand, threw everything away, like all the cell phones that ended up in the back of the graveyard drawer the day newer, cooler models were released on any carrier. I would just add that carrier and never bother to cancel the previous one. I was a pathological future addict, running from my past, and he was the unmovable bull of now.

The three potted lemon cypress trees on the brutally sunlit windowsill were dying. We decided to replace them with something sturdier and more self-sufficient, which was how we ended up on the Web site of a cactus nursery.

"Wait. Go back," I said.

I reached over and dragged my fingers across his laptop screen to slide the page.

He rolled his eyes. "It's not a touch screen."

Was he even serious? "Then just scroll on the track pad while I touch the screen."

"Oh my God," he said under his breath.

To his credit, he did scroll, and the screen slid back a few pages to where I wanted it. So it turned out his laptop was a touch screen, after all.

With everything, there is a trade-off. With a cactus, you get the autistic brother of a houseplant, something that asks nothing of you and remains alive. The trade-off is that if you barely touch it, there is a crime scene's amount of blood. Plus, ugly. And after ten years, it might be an inch taller.

"Maybe we should just stack underwear in the window," I said. The plants were only there for privacy, and underwear wouldn't need to be watered or have its leaves dusted.

The downtown apartment was on the eleventh floor and had windows that faced south and west. Also north if you didn't mind sticking your head out the bathroom window, which I didn't. Across the street was a remarkably—in a boring way—similar building. I had a telescope so powerful I could read magazine page numbers inside those apartments, which is how I knew for a fact that our lives were infinitely more interesting and watchable than our neighbors'. Which is why we needed the privacy.

A four-poster bed sat in the center of the apartment, draped with Indian sari fabric curtains. Each wall was a different gemstone color—turquoise, jade, ruby red, amethyst purple, a couple of orange tones. A curtain of plastic ruby beads hung behind the bed, illuminated by workroom lights from the 1940s. A two-hundred-year-old cement antelope weighing almost four hundred pounds, originally a French garden ornament, peered lovingly out one window while two lamps made from antlers and quail feathers perched in another. Somehow, inside the confines of this single studio apartment, we had managed to cram an upright piano, a complete gemological laboratory, including a stereo microscope and a kiln (a kiln!), a dining table, two sofas, a desk, numerous chairs and tables, three dressers, two eight-foot cabinets filled with rare books, mineral specimens, and other assorted curiosities, along with a bench detailed with carved swan necks. The windows had large, old farmhouse shutters with peeling green paint. I bought them on eBay for an astonishingly low price; they were so authentic they looked entirely fake, faux finished to appear "rustic chic."

Our neighbors in the high-rise across the street, on the other hand, had beige sectional sofas across from large-screen televisions. Their walls were off-white. They used energy-efficient lightbulbs and sat around tapping at their iPads.

It all boiled down to this: our neighbors consumed entertainment, and we manufactured it.

"I don't think we should stack our underwear in the windowsill," Christopher told me. "It would cross the Grey Gardens line."

I made a *hmpf* noise, because didn't we cross that line when I began using the cement antelope's horns as a place to store my huge collection of jade bangles? Or uptown, where he and Zeke had been slowly turning into Big Edie and Little Edie until I performed a successful intervention?

When the cactus Web page offered nothing of interest, I returned to my phone to continue watching a period drama on Netflix, and Christopher opened an e-mail query from an aspiring writer. Several moments passed in silence before I realized, quite unexpectedly, what we needed.

"Holy fucking shit," I announced.

He turned to me.

"Google 'kumquat tree,'" I told him.

He typed it in, and I leaned over him and watched the images scroll past.

He smiled and nodded. "Uh-huh," he said in his *totally* tone of voice.

"Right?" I said.

"I like this idea. A lot." I got the eyebrow raise on *a lot*.

So there it was: we would plant a kumquat tree in the window, which of course would not do anything to solve the looming issue of botanical self-sufficiency. But this didn't matter anymore. We'd just have to remember to water them and be better plant parents, that's all.

"And we could plant tall corn plants in the other windows," I realized.

There was a brief silence. "Like, *corn* corn?"

"Sure," I said. "In those long, skinny window boxes they make for the outside. Only we could use them inside."

I saw the flash of alarm on his face. He had a falling window box incident in his past, the result of which could have sent him to Rikers Island and I would be without him.

Unthinkable.

"*Indoor* window boxes," I told him to alleviate the anxiety that I knew the phrase inspired in him.

"With corn," he said again, thinking about it, trying to picture it.

"Real corn. That grows all the way up to the ceiling," I said. The hard sell.

He smiled. He loved me. But there was no way he was going to let me plant corn in the window, I could see it on his face.

Months went by, and we fell into a comfortable routine of sneaking around. We spent all our time together, except for the many hours of daily separation while Christopher was at work. Ever the writer, I was only starting to realize that he had other clients, who I'm sure were perfectly nice people, but they were hogging all my time with him. We found a practical rhythm for dealing with our business, which somehow became easier and more efficient. We'd always spoken with complete honesty, but now he didn't even need to spin things like "Let's make the next one a game changer" because he could go right for "Your career is in the shitter if this next one doesn't work," which I appreciated. (The delivery method, if not the message.)

We had known each other well enough and for long enough that most of the new information we exchanged was about things that had happened that day. The surprising facts about me were few, having published enough memoirs for an octogenarian and Christopher having read large chunks of them that never made it to print. He definitely had a few surprises still tucked away, but we'd known one another for a decade before getting romantically involved. We were a unique couple.

One thing we were not was official. We couldn't go public before telling Dennis, and I dreaded doing that. Christopher was still maintaining a relationship with him, but he was increasingly uncomfortable, mostly with his own behavior.

"I haven't told him a direct lie, and I don't say anything

self-serving to mislead him," Christopher told me, "but now my entire conversational style is one big all-night lie of omission."

At some point, Dennis invited Christopher to the Massachusetts house for a weekend, and Christopher made up a last-minute lie to get out of it.

"I can't go there and allow him to host me," he said. "I'm a terrible enough friend right here in Manhattan."

"I have to tell him," I said in a miserable monotone.

"He really does deserve to know. The thing is, your relationship is already so fraught that he's never going to hear this the right way. You'll lead with 'Christopher and I are sleeping together,' and the rest will be a fight."

"So what are you saying? I should write him a letter? E-mail him?"

"No, no, it definitely has to be done in person." He paused. "The thing is, I would do a much better job than you."

I let a nanosecond pass before "Really? You think so? Okay," came tumbling out of my mouth as one sentence.

"I would approach it like an agent," he said.

"Yes," I agreed, but not too eagerly, "like you're pitching a novel."

"Right." He sighed. "A horror novel."

A few weeks later, Dennis drove down with the dogs for the weekend. He arrived, dropped them off, and went to run errands and do New York things. That afternoon, I got an e-mail from Christopher that said, "We're meeting at seven for drinks and dinner."

I responded: "TELL HIM."

Christopher's instruction was to call me as soon as the deed was done and Dennis was on his way back downtown. As I waited, worry took over to the point that I couldn't even look at jewelry online. What was happening? Had Dennis thrown a glass of wine in his face? Had he shattered a bottle against the wall and cut Christopher's throat with the jagged edge? When I hadn't gotten a call by ten, I was certain this was the case. The dogs picked up on my anxiety and nuzzled into me on the bed. What if this was the last time I ever saw them? The thought made me hyperventilate. I tried to imagine how nice it would be to have an aneurysm and not have to face a future without them or any of the carnage I knew awaited.

By eleven, I was manic. By midnight, I was ready to take a cab up to find the crime scene. This could not have gone well. Five hours? Even if he didn't bring it up right away ("Cheers, good to see you, I've been fucking your ex for six months"), how could it possibly take so long?

Shortly after 1:00 A.M., Christopher finally called. The phone had barely rung before I grabbed it and said, "Oh thank God. What happened? Did you tell him?"

"Oh yeah, I told him," he said.

"And?"

"And . . . it was really weird. Of course, I made sure we were both reeeeeally drunk before I brought it up."

"Was he furious?"

"No. That was the weird part. I think he was so shocked that he didn't know how to react. But he wasn't angry. He said it was going to take time to sink in. And then the strangest thing of all. After dinner, he said the same thing he's said after every meal we've ever had: 'Do you want to get a nightcap?'"

Nightcap. Of course. His inner '50s housewife needed it.

"So wait. You went out and drank more?"

"We did. I can't believe he wanted to sit across another table from me, but that's what we did." I had paused in my terror long enough to hear the thickness of the liquor on his tongue. "I poured him into his cab, and he's on his way. So. All yours! Good luck!"

Somewhere in the twenty-minute taxi ride between the Upper West Side and Battery Park City, it had sunk in for Dennis. The day before, he'd asked if he could spend the night in the apartment, which seemed intolerable to me, but could I say, "No, you may not"?

He returned to the apartment ashen and zombielike. The dogs jumped up and ran to him when he came in, but he barely saw them. He took off his shoes and lay on the very edge of the bed, as far from me as he could possibly get while still occupying the same piece of furniture.

"So," I said, "I guess Christopher talked to you."

There was silence for a moment. He cleared his throat. "I can't talk about it now."

"Okay. Well. When you . . ." I stammered.

The tensest silence of my life followed.

Dennis lay stiffly in the same position all night, though he did not sleep. When the sun had just barely risen, he got up, threw his few items in his bag, leashed up the dogs, and walked out the door without a word.

As if I had conjured the dreaded event simply by allowing it to enter my brain, that was the last time I ever saw my dogs.

Once Christopher and I were free to tell people we were a couple, I was able to focus on the happiness of that future even as I mourned my past. I was furious with Dennis for masquerading as someone who cared about me and furious with myself for not seeing through it, but the joy our friends displayed when they heard the news pulled me along.

The one blip on the happiness chart was Christopher's boss, the proprietor of the small agency where he worked. A longtime friend and previously a reasonable person, he became enraged when Christopher told him. His anger extended from his worrying we'd break up and I'd fire Christopher, to it looking bad that one of his agents was not just sleeping with a client but was a home wrecker in order to get him, to his being kept in the dark for so long. When the man dropped dead a month later, Christopher, in shock, said flatly, "I guess we know what did *him* in."

Because I missed the dogs, I decided I needed a replacement, a breed that would fit into this microspace. Walking through a pet store around the corner from Christopher's office, we noticed a sweet, sleepy Italian greyhound that was the skinniest puppy I'd ever seen. They took him out of his cage so we could play with him, and he cuddled in my arms and licked me twice with his tiny, dry tongue.

I looked up at Christopher and grinned. "Add to cart!"

He snorted. "And now we have to tell people we bought a pet store dog."

"Technically, we did rescue him from this disgusting pet store," I said.

We named him Wiley, pulled from a list of Civil War–era names, and he pranced liked a reindeer on pipe-cleaner legs. He was also shaky and agoraphobic. When strangers saw him cowering and shivering and skittering, they all assumed he'd had a dramatically abusive past. And by "all," I mean every single person who saw him. Each one felt the need to make sad faces and say, "Awwww, look at how scared he is. He must be a rescue." I quickly got to the point where I wanted to say, "Actually, no, he's a purebred, but I beat him."

Thin as a cardboard paper towel tube, Wiley turned out to be hugely rambunctious and mischievous in private. For having almost no body mass, he generated an incredible amount of heat that radiated out from beneath the layers of blankets and sheets where he'd burrow. In researching the breed, I learned that they had in fact been bred in the UK (not Italy, curiously) as royal bed warmers. This made perfect sense, given his standoffishness to grubby strangers and my being a direct descendant of King James of Scotland. So I essentially wore a crown and ruled a land, and Wiley was my servant.

Because things were going so well and I was happy, I just couldn't shake the feeling that if a taxi didn't career onto the sidewalk and crush me, it was going to be something else just as bad, and soon. I felt stalked by doom. Christopher left for his office in the morning, and I stayed on top of the bed, laptop poised, panic ticking.

I never left my apartment except for the briefest and most necessary trips to the small grocery store exactly one block to the west. I thought of myself as *reclusive*. But I'd actually become something a little closer to agoraphobic.

I stopped taking Adderall, the legal speed, crystal meth with a better name, and I started to feel crazy. Meaning drained out of my life. A drudge appeared, a thick glue that fused me to the empty moment, preventing me from filling it with any activity except my circles of worry. But I hated being on psychoactive drugs like my insane mother had been all of my life, so I was determined to stick it out. I needed to give my brain chemistry a chance to settle back into whatever decrepit state was its normalcy. The Adderall had helped me, but then it seemed not to help. So maybe it had done its job and rewired something? I had to find out.

Skinny Wiley jumped off the bed; I experienced a pang. Though over a year old, he was not housebroken yet; he still had accidents. But I suspected his accidents were fully intentional, as he disliked going outside into the rain or wind or sun or weather or air. I merely called them *accidents*, because that way, I retained hope that he hadn't figured it out yet and would, eventually, learn to go outside like every other dog in the world.

But, of course, he had learned. And so had I. House-breaking had been our private little war. I would take him outside to pee, and he would fidget and look all around, as if being stalked. He would tremble and pace but not pee. When I urged him on, "Hurry up, Wiley, go ahead," he would glare at me with the most human of faces, as if to say, "Yeah, asshole, take me back upstairs, and I'll be happy to piss. I don't see you whipping it out to have a slash out here, so gimme a break." He'd simply learned it was nicer to shit on the warm bathroom floor than the cold, windy asphalt of the dog park. He was an Italian greyhound, but I rechristened him an imperial greyhound because it suited his personality better.

It did occur to me that instead of properly training him, I had succeeded merely in transferring my own phobias onto his exceptionally sensitive nature.

I worried about his chewing; he gnawed the legs off the sofa, the red lacquer Chinese side table, the zebra rug. Only the cement antelope was safe from his little monster teeth.

I worried about money, my taxes. I was criminally overdue. Why had I purchased so many antique opal, emerald, and diamond rings? Why had I invested so heavily in midcentury men's rings of chrysoberyl cat's-eye, jade, and sapphire when men didn't even wear rings anymore? I shifted part of the blame onto Adderall. It had a way of underscoring my obsessions, making them seem desperately important. I had such focus: I could spend nineteen hours looking at pictures of gemstones or rings online and still have dreams about them after I fell asleep.

I also blamed my grandmother Carolyn. She'd been dead for years, though I missed her daily, more now in fact than when she was alive and placing tomatoes in her windowsill to ripen.

One of my sharpest, finest memories is of being six or seven and sitting beside her as she steered her Cadillac Fleetwood along the highway in Atlanta, my eyes fixed on her bony fingers, glittering with rings of jade, coral, and diamond. My mother and father sent me south to stay with my grandparents when things between them became particularly explosive, so I associated my grandmother and her rings with comfort and safety.

I had been buying rings and jewelry for my entire life.

When Christopher sold my first book, I spent the advance money on two things: a signed first edition of Anne Sexton's *Live or Die* and a white-gold ring from Cartier.

The manuscript for my current book was late. This was because I seemed unable to write. When I typed, only gibberish came out. But if I didn't turn in a manuscript, there would be no money. And what money remained was swiftly spiraling down the drain. My solution to the rising panic I felt over my writing was to search out jewelry. At the time, each one seemed absolutely essential. *I may end up homeless,* I thought, *but at least I'll be wearing a vintage platinum ring set with an emerald from Colombia's legendary Muzo mines.*

When you're lathering yourself in the shower and you find a lump, it's always cancer. Before it turns out to be a pimple or a mosquito bite you forgot about or some other not much of anything, it's cancer.

Yesterday, when I felt a swollen gland along my inner

thigh, I felt blinded with certainty that it was lymphoma. Christopher had lymphoma in 2008; it began as a lump in exactly that spot. Because he was essentially a survival expert, I decided not to tell him what I found.

But after I dried off and climbed onto the bed in which we slept, socialized, and worked, the beating wings of anxiety pushed the words out of my mouth.

"Where is it?" he asked.

This was not what I was expecting him to say. I had been prepared to hear, "It's nothing." Instead, he wanted specifics.

I dreaded this. I pulled the waistband of my shorts down to reveal the flat part near the hip, which I'm not sure even has a name, except it's where lymphoma lives.

"Here?" he said, pressing on the gland.

That he'd found it so quickly was, as far as I was concerned, confirmation. There would be no need of a biopsy.

"That's nothing," he said.

"Nothing?"

He said, "No. Are there any cupcakes left?"

I told him I thought there might be two or three. "Why is the pimple always cancer for me?"

He laughed and told me it's because I'm a catastrophist. Then he brought up the rooftop swimming pool. "Remember?" he said, teasingly.

Yeah, I remembered. Because, *crazy*.

We'd been in bed watching a movie, and there was this sound. It was loud and came from above us somewhere in the building. We looked at each other, and he kind of shrugged and went back to the TV, but I continued to stare up at the ceiling. Eventually, he noticed and said, "What are you looking at?"

His question had snapped me right out of it. I'd been trapped inside this superrealistic fantasy where the rooftop pool was crashing through all the floors, and in my mind, I was imagining a huge hole ten feet from the bed and extending all the way to the door, blocking our exit. I imagined this hole plunging eleven stories, straight down to the ground. So when he asked, I was actually trying to remember how to tie secure knots so that I could knot the sheets together and hang them out the window, praying they would be long enough to get us onto the sidewalk. Then I realized I would have to secure the sheets to the iron bed, because when tugged, it would smash up against the window frame but not fit out it, so we'd be secure. This played out like a warp-speed movie in my mind, and I was actually feeling sweaty and nervous, stressed out.

"And do you remember what I said to you when you told me about this crazy disaster porn?"

I nodded.

He reminded me again, poking my shoulder. "I told you, there is no rooftop pool."

I swatted away his gloating hand and said, "Yeah, but it *could have been* the roof deck that came crashing down; it didn't have to be a pool."

He rolled his eyes, but I could tell he was also impressed. "You're the master of disaster."

Several days later, we climbed into a 2001 Acura belonging to our friends Laura and Leslie, and the four of us drove to see Punch Brothers, a bluegrass band so brilliant, its lead member won a MacArthur grant. I spent most of the concert at the Tarrytown Music Hall, a Queen Anne–bricked playhouse built in 1885, feeling that it was probable the balcony, where we were seated, would collapse on the people below due to the uproarious foot pounding that was going on.

In my mind, I frequently see these movies of terrible things that may happen. When I was young, I considered this to be both a side effect of my unstable and rather terrible childhood but also the very reason I was able to survive it. When the *Titanic* went down, I would have already been sitting in the first lifeboat ten minutes after we boarded.

The thing is, the *Titanic* doesn't always sink. In fact, it almost always stays afloat.

So I imagine terrible things in advance of their occurrence to prepare myself. And when I was small, it's true that one terrible thing after another did happen. And it was good, in a sad way, that I had been waiting, bags packed, ready for anything, no matter how sharp the blade. But as an adult and one with some success, the terrible things happened with less frequency.

I've never been able to stop the blockbuster disaster film from playing on an endless loop in my mind.

I see the terrible coming, whether it is or not.

In many ways, book tours are like stepping onto a factory conveyor belt. My publisher arranges all the travel, including car services to pick me up and drop me off. Things generally flow smoothly, but once in a while, there's a glitch. It's usually something small like having the wrong address for a radio station, so I'm always ready for that. What I don't expect is a tiny glitch that changes my life, so of course that's exactly what happened.

I had a Friday morning television interview in Chicago, and my driver had expected more traffic than we encountered, so I arrived at WGN-TV studio about an hour and a half early. I went into their spooky, empty cafeteria, sat on one of the plastic chairs, and stared at the wall-mounted television. Rachael Ray was making deviled-egg-and-bacon sandwiches, and I remember thinking, *That girl needs to stand up straighter, or the countertop on her set should be taller.* When I reached my threshold for food preparation demonstration broadcasting, I pulled out my phone and started reading. When I next looked up, it was probably forty-five minutes later, and what I saw on the screen caused me to freeze. It was a close-up of a puppy with ears that stuck almost straight out from its head. I stood and walked over to the TV. Rachael Ray was gone; this was local. And that could only mean one thing: that puppy with the Flying Nun ears was in the very building.

Sure enough, the segment featured three women volunteers from A Heart for Animals of Huntley, Illinois. They were on WGN to find homes for these three Corgi-shepherd mixes. When the segment ended, I walked into the hallway and waited for the stage door to open. The women appeared, each holding one of the puppies. I casually strolled the length of the hallway where, of course, others had gathered to fuss over the dogs.

One of the women handed me a puppy as though she'd been expecting me. I took it in my arms. It was soft and warm, and the heaviest part of the entire puppy was its paws. I could actually hold puppies for a living, so I lost track of time. I had to hand the dog back in order to be attached to a mic and shuffled onto the set for my interview.

When I was off the air several minutes later, the women were still there with the puppies in their arms. So I lingered. And I spotted the puppy with the sticking-out ears. Somehow, though I don't even remember asking, I ended up with that puppy in my arms.

The next thing I knew, I was standing with him in front of a giant clown having my picture taken. (Seriously, WGN was the original broadcaster of Bozo the Clown, so they have a twenty-foot-tall likeness in their lobby.) I had to leave, because I was already going to be late for my radio interview (which I did, actually, miss), so I handed the puppy back.

In the car, I looked at the photo and sent it to Christopher. But as I looked at the shot, I saw that the puppy and I each had the identical semipathetic expression on our faces. We matched, exactly. In my note with the picture, I said to Christopher, "I feel I have made a grave mistake and should have the car turn around to get the puppy. He is already a TV star, and some unworthy person is going to snatch him up."

I was joking, of course. We had been discussing how a second dog might make Wiley slightly less of an unsocialized freak, but I knew Christopher would laugh and say, "Yeah right. Finish your tour, and we'll see about another puppy when you get home."

Instead, though, he contacted the ladies at A Heart for

Animals and made the necessary arrangements to adopt the puppy and have him flown to New York on Sunday.

I said, "You're not just doing this because of me, are you?"

"Are you kidding? I found the segment online, and I was laughing so hard. He's the one in the middle whose eyes kept following the camera, right? He's perfect and great. Totally ours."

If there hadn't been a glitch and I hadn't arrived at the TV studio over an hour early, there wouldn't be a puppy with Flying Nun ears waiting for me when I got home a week later.

Christopher's most dominant feature was his laugh. He laughed frequently and hard; the laugh of a shaggy cartoon dog, full of gusto and physical shaking. In all his childhood pictures, he is either smiling or teetering on the edge of hysterics.

He only had one mood.

I had known him for thirteen years and never tired of his mood. It did not swing. He was in a great mood when he woke up each morning, and he would be in a great mood when he came home from work in the evening. The single exception would be while he watched sports. During the World Series, he was liable to scream at the TV, "No, no, no, *come on*! What is this, *The Bad News Bears*?" The only time I ever saw Christopher genuinely close to rage was during the US Open.

I, too, had one primary emotion: worry.

That's why we work, I thought. My endless cycles of

obsessive dread and worry were just a joke to him, something to laugh at. "You're getting a cavity filled, not having a lung transplant."

I hadn't been able to write a good, solid word for three years, and I hadn't read a book for almost ten years. As a writer, these were difficult things to admit. I was such a good monkey for so many years, cranking out the books like they were hot dogs. Though as a writer, I felt totally comfortable mixing metaphors involving simians and ballpark franks.

When I realized at almost exactly the same time that the man I had built a life with did not love me and I myself had loved Christopher from the very start, a biological event occurred, something new became alive in me. The shell that had contained it ruptured. I hemorrhaged cash.

Was it my own trust in myself that was broken? Dennis had been my source of comfort. The smoke and mirrors of it was he hadn't been that at all. I had been comforted by my belief in who he was and what we were. But the bald facts had never been a safe place for me. My comfort and sense of security had been an illusion, a work of my own creation.

This knowledge in no way led to understanding. My malformed, childlike brain knew only that it felt safe for the first time in its life, yet suddenly there was more terrible chaos than it had ever known. The difference was, in the center of the spiraling whirlpool as everything was sucked away from me, there was Christopher, the single thing I had told myself I never loved but always had. There was proof:

the best thing in life and the worst thing you can imagine can happen—and do—at exactly the same moment.

It's not that I couldn't write any longer. It's that I was alive, and it was hard for me to pull myself away from it.

When you lose one thing, it's like there's a contraption in the sky that blinks awake and starts counting and displaying all the other things you lost but hadn't realized, all the things that are teetering on the edge.

Christopher had cancer and AIDS, and every moment was so precious that I had to think about motives. Wasn't it just a little bit true that I wanted him to give up the place on Seventy-Ninth Street so that he would be stuck here with me in the tiny studio with the dogs and the sun coming through the antique farmhouse shutters? Slats of brightness and shadow, wallpaper made out of sheet music, walls the color of gemstones, two dogs, a bed draped like a Bombay whorehouse, a bookcase with glass doors that was filled with my abominations: diamond rings, South Sea pearls, chryso-beryl cat's-eye rings in eighteen-karat gold, two emeralds from the ancient Muzo mines in South America, jadeite beads in apple green from the old mountains in Burma, un-treated, so rare it took me forty-seven years to even see a strand this fine.

I wore my finest piece of jade around my neck. It is the color of an emerald from the old mines in South America and so translucent it's almost transparent. It was carved by a thoughtful hand in the 1930s, and you can see art deco it-self in the lines. Sometimes when I look at it in the middle of the night, I can feel the slightest pinprick of tears sprouting in my eyes. The closest I come to crying is this.

My most precious things. I needed them. I wanted them all within arm's reach. So yes, I admit that much. It did not make me sad to think of Christopher leaving his twenty-eight-year-old apartment behind. It did not pain me to imagine him working beside me on the bed where I worked.

How much life did we get to have together? If I believed in God, and I wish I did, I would pray right now: two long lives, all the rest of them. But what if we had less? What if there were only ten years ahead of us? What if only five? What if one? What if not even that?

Or perhaps I would die first, struck down by an SUV while I was examining my ring in the sunlight at the crosswalk.

I keep a gemological binocular microscope on the dresser beside the bed so that I can lean over whenever I like and stare deep into the heart of any gemstone. I could study the swirling horsetail inclusion inside a demantoid garnet from the Ural Mountains or spot a glass-infused ruby by the air bubbles trapped inside.

There was a time before diamonds were widely known when pearls were considered the rarest, most precious gems in the world. In many portraits depicting early monarchs, the crown features pearls instead of diamonds. But if you dropped a pearl into a glass of vinegar, it would eventually disintegrate.

That was what time did to life: it disintegrated it. Time

was like low-grade acid that slowly worked against the shell of everything, splitting it apart into powdery nothingness.

Alcohol did this, too. Whole sections of my life were splashed with liquid from a bottle and were now undecipherable, smeared and forever unreadable. Which I supposed was fine, because the past had been swallowed and digested. One must not write letters or leave voice mail for the pork chop one had for dinner four years ago.

My neighborhood was quickly transforming into something recognizable: a terrorism tourist attraction. When I moved to Manhattan in 1989, Battery Park City was new and sterile. You could practically smell the glue drying.

But along with the new World Trade Center was a new industry of tourism. The other day, I had gone across the West Side Highway to get a box of Red Bulls because they cost two dollars less at a tiny deli across the highway, and I was pretending like that made me fiscally responsible. On my way back, I came upon a group of tourists and their guide.

It would be obvious to anyone walking past that these people were tourists, probably Eastern European. The over-embellishment of stitching on the jeans was like a shrill, emphatic cry of "Designer!!!" And the jeans themselves were a shade of blue unworn by Americans or Europeans; a post-acid-wash pale blue that suggested the peeling lead paint of a cold-war maternity ward.

The colors of the assorted parkas and jackets worn by the group were also out of tune: irradiated green, paste beige, seagull-belly gray. Several of the tourists wore brand-new

Nikes, but the trademark swoosh was upside down. I supposed they were from a landlocked nation; Belarus perhaps, or maybe Slovakia. They had done their vacation wardrobe shopping at Wall of Marts, their homegrown imitation.

The tour guide was talking about fingers. I imagined he was telling them that for weeks after the 9/11 attacks, people were brushing fingers and ears and other human whatnots off the window ledges of office buildings. Such ghoulish trivia would probably be fairly obvious if you considered the situation even briefly. But here was a man making a living by taking tourists around and showing them just where certain parts and pieces had been found.

I thought, *They never should have cleaned up Ground Zero. They should have added a tram and let people ride through the smoking carnage.*

No matter how awful something is, you can always sell tickets.

The thing is, I had always loved living there by the water and the tower, never more so than during its rebuilding, its rising from the smoldering ashes. Floor by floor, the new World Trade Center rose, and I would look at it out my bathroom window as I brushed my teeth and think, *Okay, rebuilding seems possible.* I had come to this apartment after Dennis feeling ruined, and now I felt my life to be vastly superior to the one before.

Just vastly.

We were in Dayton for Christmas. Christopher's parents had been married for almost sixty years, which explained a great deal about Christopher. They met as students at Detroit's performing arts high school, the same one Diana Ross and Lily Tomlin attended. This time, we were at a hotel, but sometimes when we visited them, we stayed in Christopher's old bedroom, which still had his high school trophies on the bookshelves. A paint-by-number clown hung above the plaid armchair next to the bed.

It was a time capsule and contained no dust anywhere.

The house sat atop what in the suburb of Kettering probably qualified as a hill but which I saw more as a gentle rise. There were homes on both sides, to the rear, and across the street, and their yard sloped gently downward into the neighborhood one street over.

Christopher decided it was fine to let the dogs off the leash. I reacted as though he'd suggested we make blender drinks, strip naked except for our socks, and then run down the street, each of us holding one edge of a rainbow flag. "Are you fucking kidding?"

He told me I was being ridiculous, that this was a perfectly safe thing to do. "It's my parents' backyard," he said. Meaning: nothing bad can possibly happen to us. If I'd had his parents, it's likely I would have felt this way. But what I felt was, if they don't run into the street and get hit by a milk truck, a hawk will spiral down from the sky and lift the skinny one up off the ground and into a tree for dinner. Unleashing the dogs was the equivalent of beheading them.

When he unhooked them, they looked surprised at this sudden, unprecedented freedom and charged off down the hill. In that instant, I saw them vanishing into the distant

horizon. But Christopher called them, and they returned.
He had to speak their names five or six times, but they turned
around.

When they were close enough, I reached out and grabbed
them like they were standing on the slippery deck of a sail-
boat in exceedingly rough seas, and I snapped their leashes
back on to their collars.

In the car as we were driving back to the hotel, I was
going over what I would say if I ever spoke to him again. In
my mind, we had barely escaped complete and catastrophic
disaster. He did not understand this. My blame would crush
him like a Zamboni falling from the sky.

The thing is, the off-leash experience hadn't worked out
as well as he believed it had. My brain was currently playing the Imax 3-D film *What Could Have Happened to Wiley
and Radar*, and in this motion picture, the dogs did not turn
around when he called them. They simply kept running until they were truly and fully gone from our lives.

Knowing that I am super paranoid and irrational on the
best day did not alter my state of mind to the slightest degree. It merely reminded me that I was also constantly roiling with rage and terror.

He started laughing, a wildly inappropriate response,
while I planned the details of our ugly breakup.

"What?" I muttered.

"My mother," he said, still laughing and shaking his head.
"Do you know about the wedding dress?"

It was like being pulled from the sucking muck of quick-
sand, those distracting sidebars of his. "What wedding

dress?" I said. "What are you talking about?" I tried not to sound miserable but also resented that he was oblivious to my misery.

He told me that the family had gathered for his parents' fiftieth anniversary, and after the celebratory, wine-fueled dinner, his mom thought it would be a spectacular idea for all three granddaughters to try on her old wedding dress, which was packed away upstairs.

He was laughing harder now. "After all the girls had modeled it, she thought she'd try it on herself. A few minutes later, she came down the stairs, laughing. She turned around and said, 'I couldn't zip it all the way up, but not bad, right?'"

I could absolutely picture this. Christopher's mother at seventy could have passed for a woman in her fifties.

"Then she started twirling around, and she lost her balance and tripped on the train, and she fell right into the chair and onto me. I was trying to get her back up, and she was sort of rolling around and laughing hysterically, and I was like, oh my God, my mother is giving me a lap dance in her wedding dress."

He was laughing so hard that he should have pulled the car over. It was like driving in a sudden torrential downpour, but I was laughing almost as hard—but at him, not his story. The only reason I was not doubled over in hysterics and practically banging my head on the dash was because the warning system in my brain was telling me to prepare for a front-end collision.

It was almost enough to kill the joy, but it didn't. Because I realized, there could not possibly be a better way to die.

I became angry when I was worried, and when my worry was derailed, the anger became brittle and cracked away. I could see what was beneath it: *pretty fucking happy.*

We reached our friend Kate's place on the Carolina coast, and the beach was massive and white, and there was not another person in sight. My thinking was, *We're here for four days, so let's let the dogs get accustomed to the beach and the waves and the sand and the strange house with the strange people and then maybe before we leave, we can let them off the leash.* I showed Christopher the sixty-foot rope I had brought along.

"What in the world did you bring that for?" he asked as I slid it out of my bag.

"It's so we can tie it to their collars. It'll be like they're off leash."

He said, "Um, no, actually, it won't."

The rope was put away, a squealing rabbit with patchy hair stuffed back into the magician's threadbare black velvet bag. I submitted to the tide of reason: a person who cannot allow his or her dogs the freedom to run off leash on a beach has no business having dogs. The inner voice that told me this had pursed lips and sterling silvery hair pulled into an eye-tighteningly disciplined bun.

We walked along the beach with Kate before doing anything else. She bid us to leave our socks and shoes by the hammock and stepped into the sand. Christopher carried both dogs' leashes, and although I felt a tightening in my throat, as though a miniature being were inside my chest pulling on a flagpole's rope, I was also genuinely surprised when I saw the permanently skittery little greyhound prance; a cartoon fawn move he only pulled when he was supremely pleased. Like the time I left the kitchen and he stood on his hind legs and used his front paws exactly like human hands to pull the bacon I'd just fried off the paper towel on the counter. He sure did prance then.

He pranced now. Radar chased him. They did, indeed, frolic.

My anxiety became a castle made of sand, built so carefully and heavily but nonetheless much too close to the shore. Its walls eroded.

Kate pronounced, rather than merely said, "There is no better place for dogs than on a beach." That rang like a bell of truth.

After a long walk, during which they did not run away or into someone else's home or find somebody they would love more, we returned to the room. In the evening, Kate made the best spaghetti Bolognese I'd ever had.

The next morning, I slept late. When I finally made it to the kitchen for coffee, Christopher was barefoot, looking pleased.

"Kate just took the dogs for her walk on the beach," he told me. He went back to his reading without acknowledging that he'd just said, "Good morning! I murdered the dogs!"

It took a minute for me to speak. "So. You had Kate take Wiley, who won't even come to us when we call, without a leash?"

Still maddeningly impervious to my impending mental

meltdown, he said, "You should have seen how much fun they were having," as he went for a coffee refill. "So cute!"

An hour later, they had not returned. I had been perched at the edge of the screened porch the entire time, sweating not from the heat but from rage and terror and grief. My worst suspicions were confirmed when I saw Kate's figure approaching.

"Here she comes," I said. "And she's only got one dog."

Christopher squinted down the beach to where I was pointing. He snorted and said, "That's a man."

Obviously, jittery Wiley had rebelled and fled into the dunes. Kate hadn't come back yet because she couldn't figure out how to apologize, or perhaps she was gathering a group of Navy SEALs from the naval base nearby.

There would be a search with no results. I had accepted this.

Just as I was about to begin keening like a mother when presented with the mutilated remains of her child, Christopher casually said, "Look, here comes Kate with the dogs."

Impossibly, it was true. Radar trundled along close to Kate's fine legs. Wiley pranced.

A nameless, formless dread free-floated through my life. It attached like a cell to anyplace it could find a receptor. And the receptor was a question. Will the flight be late? Is it cancer? Was he lying all along behind my back? The answer was always briefly touched by something terrible, the worst possible outcome.

Friends had come and gone throughout my life; so had lovers, jobs, money, youth, and hair. These things had proven less durable than the leaden core of untamable doom that traveled with me. Even thinking, *How sad that only fear has followed me around all my life?* resulted in a follow-up thought: *How bad is the defect in the prefrontal cortex of my brain?*

It was tiring being me. I was tired of me.

But both dogs followed Kate back to the house, and I was lying on the convertible bed with the warm bulk of Radar beside me, his German shepherd face pressed against my ribs, Wiley folded tight for warmth in the narrow space between my shins. Christopher was on the other side of Radar, reading a manuscript and checking his Twitter feed. It was like every other Saturday afternoon, except we were at the ocean.

Suddenly, it felt like a lead dental cape had been lowered over me. *I cannot see myself ever walking along a beach unencumbered*, I thought darkly.

Was it that way when I was drinking? It seemed I was a great deal freer when I was drunk. The magnetic dread still filled me, but if it tried to attach itself to my thoughts, it slipped away with the gallons of liquor.

It was certainly true that I made a mess of things when I was a drunk. But weren't things an even bigger wreck now? While it was also true that I accomplished many things sober that would have been impossible while I was drinking, if you cut out this middle section of accomplishment, I was living in the same neighborhood I had when I first moved to New York and drank a bottle of Absolut vodka every night. In fact, my home was an apartment directly across the street from my first. I could see it out my window. My current apartment was a studio; back then I lived in a one-bedroom. I owned now instead of renting. But as the accountant said when Christopher asked if a lien would be placed on the apartment, "That hasn't already happened?"

So there was a window in which I wrote many books and traveled the world and met many people and earned a great deal of money, and now there was the stillness of living within what remained. And I could not say for sure that my sober life was a better life. I wanted to be able to say that, but I didn't think I could.

Alcohol numbed me. But if my senses were so overly electrified, was numbing such a terrible thing?

Without alcohol, there was no escape of any kind.

Drunk, I could run along any beach with my dogs. I could throw their leashes into the waves. I could do this while singing. I could probably do this naked.

Sober, I sat with a fist in my chest, knowing they'd never return.

I was sober when I unlatched my retirement account and siphoned the money into my own checking account. I was many years sober when I purchased the $18,000 chrysoberyl cat's-eye ring, the $47,000 five-carat diamond, the imperial jade beads, and carving. I was sober each time I clicked ADD TO CART and purchased loose rubies from Sri Lanka, golden-yellow sapphires, blue zircons, strands of uncultured salt-water pearls from Basra.

The horrible thing about being sober is you lose your excuse for being so fucked up.

They should tell you this in rehab. You should have to sign a release saying you understand and are okay with it.

If I had twenty dollars left to my name, I would certainly find a humble pair of natural stone earrings on which to spend it.

I became my own private department store vintage jewelry buyer.

I harpooned my own security. And I did this while under the influence of nothing but my own substance-untouched mind.

It dawned on me that had I been drunk, I probably would have passed out during the checkout process of many an online purchase. For that reason alone, it was quite possible I would be in better financial health if I still drank to blackout nightly.

In rehab, I was told, "Your addiction will always try to talk you back into drinking." That was precisely what was occurring at that moment. I imagined jogging up the stairs and pouring myself a glass of red wine. Impossible to say, really, what the result would be of a long-lost night of drinking. But I knew what my first morning questions would be: Did I say anything awful? Did I do something terrible? And of course, to how many people must I apologize?

I had an imaginary friend as a child. I wonder now if I only believed it to be a friend and that what I formed was actually an imaginary enemy. A compressed orb of fear and reflex, positioned just behind my eyes in the center of my forehead. So that it would have front-row center seats for everything that would ever happen to me in life and could preside in cautionary judgment and alarm. "You don't need anyone else. You have me," it says. When I am presented with a plate of ocean-fresh oysters on an elegant bed of rock salt, this voice whispers just two words into my ear: "Mercury poisoning."

It was many years ago that I hired a contractor to build a house in Massachusetts. During the framing of the structure, there was one particularly thick post of wood, situated in what would become the rear of the house. The builder informed me that this beam of wood supported the full weight of the structure.

"So, if I sawed through it with a chain saw?" I asked.

He laughed and replied, "Well, the house would fall down."

It stunned me. *This wood should be stained red*, I thought. *Or it should be made of steel*. All the other wood forming the skeletal outline of the house disappeared. Only this supporting beam mattered. When the house was finished, I could not get the image out of my mind that no matter how many locks I had on all the doors, one single madman with a chain saw could make the entire house fall down if he knew just where to aim.

I have heard people talk of their own "irrational fears." But my fears are not irrational. They are just unlikely.

My house had a spine, and somebody could sever it.

This was the house I built with Dennis. After we finished construction and then decorated it and moved in, a careless plumber made an error in one connection, and the house was flooded. The floors were warped forever. I was told that if I'd discovered the leak later than I did, the whole house could have been simply destroyed. By the kitchen faucet.

I spent a great deal of time trying not to imagine this. But it was irresistible. What if I'd overslept and come downstairs two hours later? Would the lumber from which the house was built become soggy? The day the house flooded was the day I should have walked out. I shouldn't have even turned off the faucet. We had already drowned ourselves by then, and we hadn't needed a drop of water.

How many of the things I fear or dread are actually things that I want?

I was five years old but just, because we hadn't gone to Mexico yet. We were seated at an iron table with scrollwork chairs. The ground upon which the table rested unsteadily was brick. I was having a tall Coke with flaky crushed ice and a brownie that was exactly as thick as three of my fingers. The brownie was almost perfect, because one of these fingers was made out of icing and not brownie. It did contain nuts, though I was able to tolerate it by sliding them out and tucking them into my square paper napkin. In addition, when chewed by mistake, they were not quite so terrible as I expected each time.

My mother was writing with a felt-tip marker inside a blank black book. I was with her, but we were not together. "I am not to be disturbed when I'm writing," she had trained me. She was there, but also she was not there.

I could not take my eyes off the woman several tables over who was speaking animatedly to her faceless, formless companion. The woman was all I was able to see.

I was entranced by her earrings. They dangled and glittered and fascinated me. As a result, I was doing one of the things my mother told me never to do: stare.

Quite unexpectedly, the woman rose from her table and approached ours. She smiled as she lowered herself almost to a kneel and spoke in a language I had never heard before but which instantly made me think of milky pale-blue, slate-gray, and white eggs. There was sunlight in her voice, slanted, late fall. In that moment, I wanted to belong to her.

Though I could decipher nothing she was saying in her musical and seemingly pretend language, I understood perfectly: love.

She reached up to her earlobe and slid the wire out. The gold was like a thin line of summer. She took my left hand and wrapped the stem of the dangling earring once around my middle finger and then carefully again, forming a ring. A crimson stone, cut with facets that shone white. She inspected her work and looked pleased as she stood and nodded to my mother, who had looked up from her notebook and was smiling. The woman's blond straight hair hung halfway down her back, and it swayed as she strode away. I looked down at my new ring, and the gold streak glinted, sparking the stone, which sang red.

From that moment forward, I found comfort in gemstones and jewelry. When I was bullied in the fifth grade for my tallness and strangeness, my reward would be a silver ring with a protective bar of turquoise set horizontally across the front.

There was much bullying; there were many rings.

Summers, I was flown to Lawrenceville, Georgia, to spend time with my grandparents. My grandmother wore a large oval jade stone the color of asparagus. It rested in a woven basket of gold. When her hands gripped the knobby steering wheel of her Fleetwood and the light hit the jade stone just right, it looked as though it was filled with juice, and it made my mouth water.

The earrings she wore around the house were set with rubies. "They come from the Orient," she told me. "Your grandfather brought them back from Burma."

The name *Burma* sounded irresistibly appealing to me, smoky and also sweet, like the dusty sticks of incense my mother planted in the potted trees in the living room. Almost as exciting as the scent were the wispy loops of smoke they produced.

"Where does jade come from?" I asked my grandmother.

"Why, from the same place in the Orient as the rubies," she told me. "Isn't that something?"

I agreed that it was quite something.

"Don't you wish you were growing up in a place where you could dip your hands down into the dirt and pull out a ruby or a nice piece of green jade?"

I wished this more than anything else, more than my parents being killed in a plane crash, which was among my primary wishes.

In my town of Shutesbury, Massachusetts, we had only two different varieties of rocks: tan rocks that sometimes had brown freckles and other rocks the color of a car's exhaust pipe. We were starving to death for beautiful things to look at that were not gray or brown or tan. "We have leaves," I told my grandmother. "Red and gold."

She looked at me significantly. "But only in the fall," she reminded me. "And then they die and turn brown and fall onto the ground, and you have to rake them up."

Raking leaves was the opposite of ruby earrings or a jade ring. Raking leaves was possibly the meanest thing life made us do.

I was in my midforties, so I should not have been surprised when my almost-seventy-year-old uncle survived cancer only to die the following year of a lung disease. His wife was also dead within the year. This loss did not seem possible or even real at all. I was leveled by it. I felt that I would have drunk if only I had the energy to do so, but I did not. Instead, I placed an iolite gemstone under the microscope and peered into its soul.

Looked at from one direction, it was clear and colorless except for the vaguest silvery hint, like water in a stainless steel bowl. But when I rotated the stone, it was suddenly the same definitive blue of a sapphire from Kashmir or Ceylon. This was called *pleochroism*, when one stone will appear as two or even three different colors, depending upon the angle.

Much of life was like that. It was a relief to be sober. It was also a burden and a great unfairness.

Death, I had observed, displayed no such pleochroism. It was only one thing.

Diamonds appeared oily upon magnification. Rubies were busy inside. Sapphires sometimes appeared to contain a galaxy, and emeralds could blind you with green. Opals reminded me of a beehive. Sometimes jade looked like sticky rice, and inside some alexandrites, it appeared to be raining.

Was it a universal truth that the closer you looked at something, the more you would see but the less you would understand what you were looking at?

My first emotion of the day upon waking was anxiety. Buying a jade bangle online or an antique carved jade pendant would alleviate this anxiety almost instantly, I knew, but I had already spent all the money I ever earned on jewelry, so I was forced to read a book, which felt like a punishment that was only slightly self-inflicted.

As I turned the page of the book, my eye caught a flash of perfect, midnight blue from the massive sapphire of my platinum pinky ring.

I glanced down at the ring and thought, *Pinky rings are kind of tacky.* But I also knew that I, myself, was somewhat tacky. So in no way did I feel the need to remove this ring. I paid $9,000 for it and could probably have taken it over to Forty-Seventh Street and gotten $4,000 in cash.

Then I could spend the next two weeks obsessively searching for an untreated piece of jade jewelry by searching my vast online resources. It was possible that after looking at several thousand images of items for sale, I might locate that single jade stone that I could tell just from the picture had not been chemically treated. Dyed or polymer impregnated jade was very difficult to distinguish from the valuable untreated variety, but I had, as they say, the eye. And I was almost never wrong.

That is what I wanted to do, but instead, I remained rooted to the chair. I put the book down, picked up my laptop, and began writing.

I used to love writing.

In fact, I used to require time to write every day. If I did not write, I could feel mental illness flare up and spread within my mind like a rash.

When did I begin to detest it? I had actually considered attending a barber school in Tribeca, because trimming the nose hairs of bankers seemed a far preferable way to spend my time than writing. Writing—especially if one is a memoirist—is dangerous, because it can lead to self-awareness. And I did not want self-awareness. I wanted gems. Or cocktails. Or sex. Or anything, really, except a book or anything having to do with books. I was feeling petulant, and the fact that I was no longer allowed to drink seemed profoundly depressing.

I knew that when Christopher came home from work, my misery would be lifted. I also knew this was the sure sign of a mentally unstable person. But I had finally reached the age where mental health was no longer a goal. Relief from my own foulness of mood was the only goal.

Christopher was wearing royal-blue drawstring shorts and nothing else. His blond hair had taken on a silver sheen from the sun, his skin was rich and dark, and the hairs on his legs and arms and chest sparkled.

There was a charcoal grill outside, and we loaded it with steaks and corn, unhusked.

There were three bedrooms at our rented villa, and we used them all. We took a great many naps, often in the middle of the day.

We drank lemonade from sweating glasses filled with ice. We swam naked in the pool. He lay on the inflatable yellow raft, and I steered him through the water.

Anytime I wanted to, I could lean right over and kiss him anywhere I chose. He always let me. He always loved it.

He hadn't shaved since we arrived on the island of Saint John four days ago, so each day he became a slightly different man. And each day I thought, *He's more handsome today than he was yesterday.*

When he finally shaved his face, I was hit with a sweet pang in the center of my chest, because I realized I had missed that face.

We drove to the beach and were dive-bombed by a seagull, and we wondered, "Is Tippi Hedren still alive?"

I thought, *This is how it feels inside the right decision.*

We were more than halfway through our ten-day vacation when I turned to Christopher, who was gripping the wheel of the Jeep and driving along the winding, climbing road. Suddenly, I recognized him. How could I have not seen this before?

"Oh my fucking God. You're the Jeep Guy!" I shouted.

"What? What?" he said, checking his rearview mirror, shooting me a glance like, *Did I hit a goat or something?*

Of course he was Jeep Guy. It was so blindingly obvious that I had missed it all along.

I said it again, half laughing and half shouting, manic from my epiphany. "*You.* You are totally him! I've had recurring dreams about you for years and years and years, and I only just *now* realized it, watching you drive."

But this made zero sense to him, because he didn't know about my Jeep Guy dreams; I'd never mentioned them.

Plus, the moment I said the words *recurring dreams*, I could see that I'd lost him. Christopher has a zero-tolerance policy for the retelling of dreams.

"Oh no, please don't," he said. Then he added, "I mean, I'm glad if my driving makes you happy, and you're perfect for me in every way, but the dream thing is just beyond my ability to comprehend."

I smiled at him. My cheeks actually stung with the authenticity and size of my grin. But I barreled through and told him about Jeep Guy, anyway. "I mean, I never even liked or dated rugged blond guys, and yet I had these dreams, and now, here I am with you—and you're that guy!"

His water bottle was crammed between his legs, so I grabbed it and took a sip. I poked him on the shoulder. "Oh my fucking God." Poke, poke, poke, poke, poke.

He gave me crazy-person side eye, but he didn't swat my hand away from his shoulder or take back his water bottle, and I realized I could do anything to him and he would never hate me. I could never drive him away, spoil things between us, or otherwise sour things in his eyes, because he already knew how horrible I could be, yet he loved me, anyway.

The truest thing was, I just plain worshipped his ass. I also knew that in my twenties if some guy had said, "I worship you," I would have smiled politely, suddenly "remembered" a dental appointment, and then never fucking called him again. Yet when we arrived back at the villa with heavy shopping bags of steak, corn on the cob, and ice cream, I said exactly those words to him, and he smiled and then laughed, utterly pleased.

"I am so glad," he said.

"But I really do," I continued with some anxiety. I needed him to understand. "No . . . I mean, I actually worship you, just every aspect, every detail. The hair on your legs is like fireworks. I could stare at it for hours." I wanted him to know how lower brain stem my attraction was, how deeply rooted and complete, how obsessive and terminal.

"I know you do," he told me. "Can you hand me the butter?"

After grilled steaks, we stripped off our clothes and walked outside. The pool wasn't huge, but it was amazing, sitting on a deck that overlooked a couple of miles of palm trees and then nothing but the blue Caribbean beyond. When I next glanced at Christopher, he was already airborne, having ejected himself from the edge of the pool straight out in shockingly perfect form so that he seemed to hover in the air above the water before arching himself directly into it.

He was smiling when he surfaced for air at the other side of the pool. "You should come in. It feels great," he said.

I was staring at him in open bewilderment. "So wait. How could I know you for like ten years and be *with* you for more than *one* year and yet not know you could do this?"

"Do what?" he asked, swiping his wet hair out of his eyes.

"Um, diving like that?"

"Oh, that," he laughed. "Yeah, I was a swimmer when I was a kid. I can't believe you didn't notice all the trophies in my old bedroom at my parents' house. Come on, get in," he said, slapping the water.

I walked down the steps into the pool, trying to look cool as I checked for dead snakes lurking in the corners. I dived beneath the surface and opened my eyes underwater. I swam toward him and grabbed his dick as I broke the surface to find he was already laughing.

The fired-clay tile floors of our villa were cool underfoot, and the bed was carved wood with four posters, hung with white mosquito netting that looked like a billowing wedding veil. At some point before the sun went down, we'd have to climb into the Jeep and drive on the wrong side of the road into town to buy essentials for the evening: steaks, corn on the cob, avocado, and mineral water.

I was reading a book about the Hope Diamond. Christopher was reading *Billboard*. We were both wearing shorts and nothing else. When he stood up to walk to the freezer for more ice, I watched the way his heavy penis swayed in his shorts, and I got up and followed him.

When I wrapped my arms around him, he laughed.

"You used to moan when I came up behind you like this," I told him. "Now, you just laugh."

He turned around. When he opened his mouth to say something, I kissed him. He laughed again.

"Oh, okay," I said. I could tell he was not in the mood. I felt slightly sad, but that's the way it was. I reminded him, "We used to have a lot more sex."

He looked at me like, *Are you even real?* "We had sex three times today," he told me. "That's more sex than most people have in a whole week. Some in a month."

When he put it like that, it did seem like I couldn't complain even though I wanted to. I felt like if we were standing before a judge, there was no way on earth the judge would side with me.

A few months before, Christopher had done the math. We'd had a lifetime's worth of excellent sex in the first year we were a couple. We front-loaded. I'd already asked him this question many dozens of times, but I asked it again now, fresh. "Would you marry me right now?"

"Yes," he said, laughing.

"But I'm serious. Would you?"

"Yes," he said, repressing a laugh.

"Are you sick of me yet?" I pestered.

"No," he laughed.

"Will you ever get sick of me?"

He cocked his head to the side in make-believe thought. "Well . . ."

———

When we returned from vacation, I was overwhelmed by all the daily life things that needed to be done: the apartment was filthy and needed to be cleaned, I had to write a bunch of checks, I needed to get back to my writing, I also had to make an appointment with the dentist because I was almost positive one of my crowns was cracked.

These were exactly the sorts of things that I used to run away from by drinking. Ordinary tasks have always overwhelmed me.

But I had no desire to drink now. There was nothing in my life I wanted to obliterate, not even the crappy stuff.

I was wearing a three-piece, pin-striped suit and trying not to scuff my black shoes as I shoved my way through the aggressively revolving glass door of the Marriott to meet Christopher's parents in the lobby.

When his parents stepped from the elevator, I saw them before they saw me in the crowded lobby. I wanted to call out, but I suddenly wasn't sure what to call them. *Mom* and *Dad* seemed somehow forced and awkward. Shouting out their first names also seemed weird, but then *Mr. and Mrs. Schelling* would be worse. I settled on "Hey!" while waving my arms in their direction.

"Oh, hey!" his dad said, smiling and giving me a hug. I kissed my mother-in-law on the cheek and told her she looked beautiful.

I led them outside, and we climbed into the back of a cab. "Fifty-Fourth and Eighth," I told the driver. I was taking two

280 | Augusten Burroughs

septuagenarians to 54 Below, a Manhattan nightclub in the basement of the former Studio 54, where their son would be playing piano.

Here's another thing they do not tell you in rehab: if you are an alcoholic and you stop drinking alcohol, every drink you order in a restaurant for the rest of your life will arrive with a straw in it.

So there I was at a legendary disco-and-drug den, drinking Diet Coke, the single worst liquid ever invented. This was the closest I would ever get to that legend, and my drink had a straw.

The upside was that the show was phenomenal. Christopher was the musical director and accompanist for his friend Anne, an amazing singer and actress. There was a standing ovation, and for a moment, I was happier than I had ever been in my life. Christopher was wearing a black-and-white Versace jacket with black pants, and his mustache looked like a horseshoe, and he seemed famous but wasn't. All those years he'd been just my agent there had been hidden under his clothing a concert pianist, a diver, a World Series watcher, and a great body with numerous impressive attributes. In fact, each day, things were revealed to me casually and often by accident that seemed incredibly essential for me to know, things I should have already known. Like, he could sing. I didn't even know he was color blind until six months into the naked part of our relationship. I, who had written dangerously close to a dozen books about myself, simply could not conceive of a person who didn't just blurt it all out.

Christopher's mother leaned over and said, "Those music lessons were worth every penny." She was beaming.

Christopher's dad looked like he may well explode in tears.

That was when I decided there was no reason they couldn't be my parents, too. I had been cursed with the worst parents in the world, and I'd suffered through them for decades. Now that I had found two of the very best, it seemed foolish to let them get away.

The dogs crowded us to the edges of the bed when we slept, even though it was a king-sized mattress and the dogs themselves were not huge. It seemed at night they grew to the size of a third, tall person with strong, pushy limbs.

So one morning, I suggested we add a second bed. "A twin, at the foot of the king." I told him, "Remember in the 1970s? Maybe your mother didn't do this, but mine made a sofa out of a twin bed by using pillows and Indian bedspreads."

Christopher paused in the bathroom doorway, holding his coffee cup. "Yeah," he said, "if we're going to imitate one of our mothers, let's make sure it's yours. That's a really good idea." His mom had been a schoolteacher in Ohio; mine was a mentally ill poet whose psychiatrist raised me in exchange for her child-support checks.

Christopher said, "Plus, if we get a twin bed, that's where I'd end up sleeping while you and the dogs hog the king."

That night, I had a dream that Christopher was just a dick. He was a total asshole to me. I woke up in a foul mood.

"I can't believe you're mad at me for something I did to you *in a dream*," Christopher protested.

His incredulous laugh was different from his normal laugh, and I suspected I might be the only one who got to see it.

"Don't even speak to me," I said.

After five minutes, I said, "But I would marry you, even though you were just awful to me."

On April 1, 2013, Christopher and I took the ferry to Staten Island and stood before a dignified and genuinely funny city hall clerk, while down in Washington the Supreme Court was considering two watershed cases. Gay marriage was seriously trending.

As we walked out the front door of city hall, Christopher turned to me and exclaimed, "You're my husband!"

I smiled, because this was true. I was his husband and he was my . . .

Christopher's smile faded, too. "Wait," he said. "That makes me the wife."

Since I had been thinking the same thought at that moment, this confirmed that I had married the right person. But what he said was true. I tried reversing the roles by calling Christopher "my husband." And sure enough, in my mind's eye, I immediately became Tippi Hedren in *The Birds*: pea-green suit, blond chignon, heels.

I couldn't call Christopher my husband, because saying it made me feel like a cross-dresser. And believe me, I do not judge cross-dressers. But I lack the motivation to dress properly as a man, let alone an archetypal woman with layers of accessories. I have needed new sneakers for four months. How hard is it to go buy a pair of sneakers? Apparently, very.

Likewise, I don't have anything against wives, but surely I don't need to elaborate on the bullying of gay boys for being effeminate, forcing us into the caveman stance of "I ain't no damn wife."

So on this gay day, when I experienced firsthand what I believe is a civil right, instead of feeling triumphant and proud, I felt tricked.

"Getting married took away one of our words," I said.

We had previously referred to each other as *boyfriend*. Age inappropriate to some, but it did just fine. *Partner* sounds cloyingly, politically correct, or as if we work at a law firm. In *spouse*, I mostly hear "S.mouse," the name of Chris Lilley's blackface teenage rapper in *Angry Boys*. And it's stiff and formal and a little heavy in the sibilant *S* department. The best suggestion came from Liz, one of our witnesses at the ceremony, a brilliant contraction of boyfriend and husband: boyband. We're all word people, so this made us laugh, yet there was an unavoidable whiff of "I married an old man who thinks he's in One Direction," which is when I stopped laughing.

Boyfriend has become the perfectly acceptable term for an unmarried adult man in a relationship. It's cute, even as it grossly exits the wrinkly mouth of a middle-aged bald guy. And Christopher is a man unafraid to post on Twitter, "I'm only one Demi Lovato tweet away from an Amber Alert!" So though he's even older than I am, *boyfriend* comes naturally to him. Now, with our shiny wedding rings glinting in the sun, we'd lost a word forever.

Language Police 1, Gay Marriage 0.

We eloped on April Fools' Day because we are both, in fact, fools. We didn't tell anyone all week, and then midway through Christopher's fiftieth birthday party on that Friday, we surprised the guests by announcing that they were actually at a wedding celebration. The applause and cheers in the room were spontaneous and deafening. That, people, is what love sounds like. One by one, his friends came up to me and congratulated me but also made me know, in no uncertain terms, that if I ever fucked up and hurt him, that would be it.

I just could not stop smiling. I was Kate Middleton, the commoner marrying the prince. And I was totally okay with that. I was more than okay with that. I was born for it.

For the rest of the party, we were asked three questions repeatedly: "Where are you registered?" "Are you going to have kids?" and "Where are you going on your honeymoon?"

When we gave the answers "Nowhere," "No," and "Nowhere," I was able to count cavities in people's mouths, they were so astonished. The implication was if you weren't getting the Williams-Sonoma steak knives or purchasing a baby or going to Saint John, why did you marry at all?

The one element I got absolutely right was our wildly inappropriate rings. As a gemologist and lifetime jewelry collector, I chose them both. Most self-respecting men would not wear diamond rings as large and flashy as these. We've often joked (because we're deadly serious) about what "bad gays" we are, and with no big ceremony, no gifts, no trip, and no children, we confirmed it. Our wedding was apparently about jewelry, which is gay, but bad gay.

Our young and deeply attractive friends Eric and Nick are good gays. They married last summer on a lush, emerald-green lawn in the Hamptons. They wore matching cotton suits of the palest, most pleasing shade of blue imaginable. They have wonderful taste, and corsages look intended for them.

If I were to wear a corsage, something bad would happen. A tiny sprig of poison oak would be mixed in with the greenery, or a wasp would fly out and sting the first wasp-allergic child I bumped into.

Another element we got right was hiring the same talented baker who made Nick and Eric's wedding cake to create ours. Theirs had a spill of fresh, colorful flowers atop it like the cover of *Martha Stewart Living*. We requested no fresh flowers; just give us the damn cake. Nick and Eric saved a piece in their freezer to have on their first anniversary. Christopher and I took the top tier of the cake and pretty much inhaled it at 2:00 A.M. after the party.

So in addition to rings, our wedding was about sugar.

And one name fewer by which we could refer to each other.

So what had we gained? Well, that's the funny thing. I

didn't expect that being married would feel any different from being unmarried. I had fought back my romantic feelings with a machete because he was my literary agent and there were a thousand other reasons my attraction to him was impossible.

But impossible is a concept that makes one's heart laugh and throw peanuts at the television. I lost my internal machete war and finally confessed in 2009 to my best friend and the only agent in Manhattan who didn't turn me down that I was in love with him.

My life was a mess in numerous ways. But I loved every dent, tear, and crack, because Christopher was now at the heart of it all. I never imagined being married would feel any better or worse than every other day with him: slightly miraculous and always exciting. It has now been fifteen years of this excitement, the last five of which have been as a couple.

But there was something else I felt walking away from our perfect-for-us civil ceremony when I realized we couldn't call each other boyfriends anymore, and husband didn't really fit.

I felt official.

For me, saying, "I am married now," was like saying, "I am lucky now." I stumbled and crashed my way into the literal arms of something I never quite believed in before: my soul mate. A man who frequently smelled like cheeseburgers and made me laugh hard every day and made me want to be worthy of being his husband.

That trumps the loss of *boyfriend* and having to withstand the silent judgment of "Huh, so you're the wife. I wondered how that worked."

Getting married felt as if the city clerk was looking at us and saying, "Admit it. Just admit it." And we were smiling and laughing because it was true, and we both knew it. So we each said, "Yeah, I do."

When he concluded, "By the power vested in me by the State of New York, I now pronounce you married. You may seal the marriage with a kiss," I kissed Christopher and then threw my arms hard around him and pressed my mouth against his ear, barely able to speak even in a whisper, and said, "I won."

"So did I," he replied.

Christopher generally fell asleep and into a rhythmic snore within about forty-five seconds of laying his head on the pillow. This had been his way since we had been together, sawing logs within the minute.

My nights were usually spent two-thirds trying to fall asleep, one-third fitfully sleeping. First, I had to kind of decompress in the pillow, which frequently meant going over whatever slight injustices I imagined I incurred during the day and fantasizing about better courses of action I could have taken. Or sometimes my mind would just turn on its own TV, and I'd get caught up in a story of my own making, though it always seemed like it already existed and I was only watching. I also worried a lot at night, mostly about my teeth and skin rashes.

But I learned that when I finally did recline and turned on my side and he rolled an arm over me, that would be the last thing I remembered. It always made me smile and not quite grunt but almost. Like a semigrunt, semilaugh. And that was it. Blackout.

So his ability to fall asleep instantly could override my tendencies toward insomnia if there was physical contact. If he stayed on his side of the bed and I stayed on mine, I'd be up all night. But when we were touching, his sleeping patterns trumped my insanity. Even when I thought it wouldn't happen.

I never had another Jeep Guy dream. But I was married to him now. As surely as this unknown-to-me man drove me up the Rockies in his beat-up rig, this identical figure had transitioned from my dream state to my bed. It was, of course, preposterous and maybe psychotic, but it was also, in fact, true.

I hardly said four words to Christopher the whole night of our wedding party. We were too busy wearing suits and pouring champagne and smiling. But late in the evening, we passed each other in his walk-through office, and his face was . . . well, you can't fake a face like that. The guy with that face was insanely in love with whatever he was looking at.

Because I was the only other person in the room, it had to be me. "Husband," he said.

"Married," I said like, *Can you even fucking believe it?*

I had to head into the kitchen for another bottle, and he

was headed to the bedroom to get somebody's coat. But I had to ask him to make sure.

"Are you steeping in regret?"

"Totally not. You're perfect for me," he said, sounding postgame happy, and then he cracked up. I could still hear him laughing as he walked down the hallway.

I was standing behind him, my hands in the front pockets of his jeans. We were at a New Pornographers concert in Williamsburg, and I liked that we were standing so close to the speakers I could feel the music on the surface of my skin.

I didn't like the idea of coming tonight and being stuck inside such a massive, throbbing crowd, but Christopher loved this band, and I was so tired of being afraid of things, so I came, and now I was happy because this was the first time I'd ever stood pressed against him from behind like this with my hands in his pockets and music crawling all over us, and I loved getting to spend time with the back of his head because it's a really nice back of the head.

When we got home, Radar trundled over to the door, banging the walls with his twelve-pound tail, and Wiley crawled out from his burrow of covers and stood on the bed, trembling and expectant. Christopher laughed like he always does, raised his arms above his head, and called out, "Look how tall!" Wiley responded by standing on his skinny rear greyhound legs to show how tall he really was. Then Radar somehow projected himself from the floor directly onto the

290 | Augusten Burroughs

bed, where he crashed into Wiley, and the three of them formed a pileup on top of the covers.

We took off our clothes and changed into gym shorts and T-shirts. After we fed the dogs and grabbed two bottles of lemon seltzer water, we climbed onto the bed. There was a copy of *The New York Times* on Christopher's bedside table, and he grabbed it. In the Arts & Entertainment section, there was an article about *The Wizard of Oz*. He showed me the picture of Dorothy and the green witch. He chuckled as he said excitedly, "My favorite part of the whole movie is where you can see one of the yellow bricks mechanically kind of rise up and rotate so that smoke can come out."

"What?" I said, staring at him incredulously.

"It's true. I noticed it when I was a kid. I loved it. Next time it's on Turner, I'll point it out."

I looked at him, and I thought, *You are a spectacular creature.*

He shrugged. "It's funny. You'll love it," he said, and then he tossed the paper onto a chair and picked up his laptop because there was no music playing.

I started looking at antique opal pendants online because I didn't currently own a really fine black opal, and this was a problem for me.

Christopher was playing one of the German modernist composers, and after a while, I remarked, "This isn't music; it's just noise. It doesn't need to exist."

A small, pitying laugh burped out of him. "Well, it's not *noise*. But I can understand why you wouldn't enjoy it."

To be an asshole, I said, "Right, except it actually *is* just organized noise. It has no *musicality*"—a word I'd picked up from him.

Christopher is an actual musician, and I do not even know where middle C is on a piano. So normally he could just walk away from some ignorant idiot talking shit, but now he was married to this idiot, so he had to put up with it.

His laugh was the kind you make when some product fails in your hands, like the shampoo cap cracks totally off or the spatula handle snaps in half. With tolerant authority, he replied, "It's not melodic; it's definitely music."

I just grinned, because even when I really tried, it was impossible to annoy him.

He lacks the annoyance chip.

Just like he doesn't really feel melancholy, rage, or anxiety. These emotions are not part of his repertoire. It's almost an autistic quality. He mostly has one mood, and it's a very good one. I had to find somebody who was immune to me in order to have a great relationship.

All of a sudden, there is proper music: bouncy, catchy, could be '80s but isn't. I look over, and he says, "The Veronicas." This is followed by June Christy singing "Something Cool," We Are Scientists, Jóhann Jóhannsson's *IBM 1401, A User's Manual,* and Mary Schneider, whom, he informed me, "is the queen of yodeling."

He started laughing about something I'd written earlier where I said his dick was as thick as a subway pole. "I can't believe you put that in. You have to take it out." But it was really cracking him up even though it's not that funny.

I told him, "I'll change it to 'His dick was as thick as Linda Hunt's wrist.'"

This made him laugh so much harder that he was doubled over forward, and his eyes looked like, *Oh shit. This is really it. I'm gonna stroke out.* Watching him, I thought, he could actually have a heart attack and drop dead right now. Not from AIDS or from cancer but from Linda Hunt's wrist.

We settled into our laptops.

Later, an old Barbara Stanwyck movie came on. Whenever her face appeared on the screen, we both looked up.

Christopher adopted his smart-ass tone. "You'd better hope your next husband doesn't like movies in color."

I turned and looked at him. "What do you mean *next?*"

He was scrolling through album covers, because it was New Release Tuesday, the best day of the week when all the new songs came out.

He paused and met my gaze.

There was nothing sarcastic on his face, no spin. "You know," he said. "I mean, *come on.*"

I looked back at my laptop and slid my finger across the trackpad. "I know what, exactly?" I glanced back at him.

His smile had kind of faded. "You know that I'll die before you. In all probability."

I sighed. "I suppose I know it's possible. But I also know you promised not to."

Which was also true.

I said, "Or you know what? Maybe I'll go ahead and die before you. What would you think of that?"

He grinned.

Then I reminded him, "We wouldn't even be in this situation if you hadn't been such a stupid blond slut when you were in your twenties."

Christopher always laughs from his stomach, never his chest or throat. So the bed always shakes when he laughs, and sometimes he wakes up the dogs.

I slid my laptop onto the dresser beside the bed, next to my gemological microscope. A strand of glassy, untreated emerald-green jade beads from Myanmar hung from the left eyepiece. I removed the strand and slid it between my fingers for luck.

Christopher was watching me, I could feel it.

I changed my position on the bed so that I was kneeling and facing him. "I think maybe you've forgotten that you're actually still my literary agent. You work for me."

He snorted.

I went on. "I'm an extremely famous and popular person. I've been in movies and starred in an instant breakfast drink commercial. I could have been a child model, and I'm also a direct descendant of King James II of Scotland. All of which, I might add, reflects luminously well on you."

Laughing harder, he sounded like wheezy Muttley, the cartoon dog.

I informed him, "You'll die before me if I go ahead and say you're free to do so."

Then I picked up his laptop and dropped it onto his bedside table. I slid on top of him so that I was straddling his legs. I leaned in so that my face was mere inches from his.

I growled, "You are a ridiculous little man. Willful and short and hairy and old."

His eyes were sprinkled with tears, but from cracking up.

Because he did now belong to me—I earned him; I won him—and because I had memorized his every inch and knew exactly where on his left ear to place my lips and whisper, the laughter stopped at once, the circuit interrupted.

I steered my lips across his jawline and to his mouth. I kissed him. These were open-mouth kisses, young people's kisses, hungry and full at the same time, in love, at home.

I pulled back from his lips far enough to whisper, "You are my disease piñata, my Death Star, my everything."

He pulled me to him, his powerful legs, like a wrestler's, flexing beneath me. "And you," he said, "are my catastrophist."

We were walking along the Battery Park City esplanade beside the riverfront, and the dogs were straining against their leashes. There were so many stars. Which you just don't expect to ever see in Manhattan.

I said to Christopher, "Do you realize that when you look at something through an electron microscope and then you look out into the distant galaxy through a telescope, it looks the same? You can't even tell if you're looking at something tiny or something huge."

He nodded like, *That's nice.*

I smirked. "You don't give a shit about that stuff, do you?" I said.

He laughed. "No, not really."

The dogs paused to sniff the fascinating roots of the same tree.

I said, "Okay, in that case, what was A Flock of Seagulls' biggest hit?"

Christopher beamed at me as the wind blew into our faces from the river. His eyes glittered, and he replied without pausing to think about it, faster than Google, as though he'd been expecting this question all his life.

" 'I Ran.' "

I placed my hand against the side of his precious, electric face and felt the stubble beneath my fingers. I was overwhelmed with the lust and wonder of it all.

Acknowledgments

My plan had been to write a novel, not another memoir. I actually wrote *two* novels, and I didn't love them—my heart just wasn't in the writing. Then my friend Liz Stein made a suggestion that changed everything. "Why don't you write about what happened after *Dry*?" Her husband, Luke Dempsey, immediately agreed. I realized this was exactly what I wanted to write, and that's important: *I wanted to write.* Somehow, with their fresh insight, words of encouragement, and wonderful friendship, Liz and Luke have nurtured and inspired me, and I am deeply grateful.

I am also grateful to Kate Mulgrew, whose generosity, friendship, and amazing home cooking have been such blessings. Taylor Schilling came into my life at exactly the right moment, all 20,000 watts of her, full of life and intelligence and vulnerability; she has become utterly priceless to me. Anne Bobby has been both a loyal friend and a spectacular source of entertainment through her gorgeous voice, and I am so lucky to know her. My beautiful, brilliant cousins, Leigh and Meridith, remind me constantly of the importance of family, as does my wonderful family-in-law.

A lot happened while I was writing this book; my life was transformed, and I met so many inspiring and substantive people who brought me joy, including Hilary Old, Eileen Fisher, and Portia de Rossi. I also want to thank my buddies Seamus Mulcare and Jack Abramoff for making me laugh. My remarkable and supportive editor, Jennifer Enderlin, and all the good people at St. Martin's Press have been with me from the beginning. During the writing process, one of my earliest St. Martin's supporters and longtime friends passed away, so this book is presented in the memory of Matthew Shear.

Lastly, I must thank Allan R. Pearlman for keeping me out of jail.